Unshackled

Breaking Away From Seductive Spirituality

By Pastor Larry DeBruyn

Unshackled:
Breaking Away From Seductive Spirituality
Copyright © 2009 Lawrence A. DeBruyn
Franklin Road Baptist Church
51 North Franklin Road
Indianapolis, Indiana 46219
U.S.A.

ISBN—10:978-1-61623-546-8

Copies may be ordered by writing the church at the above address, or by e-mailing: www.frbaptist.org.

Contributions for the reception of this book are invited, and may be made by check written out to "Franklin Road Baptist Church," with memo designation to "Eastern European Ministries," and mailed to the church's address listed above. The suggested donation to cover the cost of printing and mailing this book is $10.00 per copy.

Book Printed by:
Moeller Printing Company, Inc.
4401 East New York Street
P.O. Box 11288
Indianapolis, Indiana 46201
www.moellerprinting.com

TABLE OF CONTENTS

INTRODUCTION AND PREFACE
As Above, So Below

Let something be stated about this book's cover with the cryptic saying, "As above, so below" on it.[1] The saying originated within a collection of fourteen ancient books known as the *Corpus Hermeticum*. According to James A. Herrick, "These Hermetic writings . . . were based on the systems of various philosophers and teachers in Alexandria, Egypt, between A.D. 150-300."[2] Dr. Herrick quotes Wayne Shumaker's statement that, "Hermeticism was basically a Greek contemplative system developed on Egyptian soil."[3] Hermeticism's goal is for human beings—via the engagement of contemplative practices (i.e., mysticism) which stimulate deeper knowledge about reality (i.e., Gnosticism)—to realize a spiraling evolution of soul into a higher state of consciousness in which they, like the mythical Hermes Trismegistus, will realize "oneness" with a divinized universe in which conscious state they will play the role of god.

As will be demonstrated in this book, Hermetic-Gnostic philosophy is establishing itself in American culture, and to some degree, in the pan-evangelical church. We note Eugene Peterson employs the phrase in *The Message*, where the Lord's Prayer reads, "Our Father in heaven, / Reveal who you are. / Set the world right; / Do what's best—*as above, so below.*"[4] (See Matthew 6:10.) Magee explains the phrase to mean:

> Everything in the cosmos is internally related, bound up with everything else . . . Divine powers understood variously as "energy" or "light" pervade the whole. This principle is most clearly expressed in the so-called *Emerald Tablet* of Hermes Trismegistus, which begins with the famous lines "As above, so below." This maxim became the central tenet of Western occultism.[5]

Hermeticism is a monistic belief that the entire of reality is one, and that this "One" is God.[6] In other words, there is no division between heaven above and earth below. All reality, the universe, is a gargantuan seamless whole. Many scientists and spiritualists presuppose that a holistic "oneness" characterizes the entire reality of whatever "is"—"down here" or "out there." On this point, we point to the paraphrasing of Ephesians 4:6, by Eugene H. Peterson. It reads:

You have . . . one God and Father of all, who . . . *is present in all.* Everything you are and think is *permeated with Oneness.*[7]

Of course, one need only read the plain words of Jesus to realize that the "Oneness" philosophy of reality utterly opposes His worldview, for He told the Jews, "*You are from below, I am from above; you are of this world, I am not of this world.* I said therefore to you, that you shall die in your sins; for unless you believe that I am *He,* you shall die in your sins" (Emphasis mine, John 8:23-24). With His words, Jesus declared that He and the Jews "emerge from two entirely antithetical realms,"[8] and that, "An abyss separates them from Him."[9] Eternal heaven and temporal earth are two separate realities. This worldview contrasts to the seductive New Spirituality which holds that the entire of reality—time and eternity, heaven and earth, light and darkness—is "Oneness."

But according to Jesus the sum is not "One." Reality is not a seamless whole. To believe that it is obliterates the distinctions of the Christian faith—that the eternal God is holy and separate from His temporal creation, that good and evil are opposite moral categories (There is sin.), that heaven and hell exist, and that Jesus came from a sphere eternally separate from earth.

Some may remember the traditional spiritual song, "He's Got the Whole World in His Hands." In part, the lyrics go:

He's got the whole world in His hands . . .
He's got the whole world in His hands.

He's got the wind and the rain in His hands . . .
He's got the whole world in His hands.[10]

According to the seductive spirituality of the New Age, God no longer has the whole world in His hands, but rather the world has God in their hands, and they are fashioning Him into whatever finite image and idol they want he, she, it, or them to be (Compare Romans 9:21.). As Christian believers who have been raised from death to eternal life in Christ, we ought to heed Paul's counsel to set our, "affection on things above, not on things on the earth" (Colossians 2:1-2).

As fine Christian scholars and writers have done far better than I, these essays make no pretense of being the final word on the Oneness Spirituality invading the soul of evangelicalism. These writings represent just one pastor's attempt to clarify how what's spiritually happening in the culture is seducing the church. By providing a ball-park glimpse of this spirituality, I hope these essays will provoke Bible believing Christians to shun the existential romanticism which is influencing the evangelical movement via such writings like Wm. Paul Young's bestselling spiritual allegory, *The Shack*.[11]

Admittedly, the novel tugs at the emotional strings of its readers, and for just that reason, the book has become a bestseller in the fiction category. I am therefore aware that I am about to tread where angels might fear. This pastor realizes he is about to enter the personal and emotional space of human hearts. We feel deeply about our lives, and readers feel deeply about this book and its author. I only ask that, as you have read Paul's book with an open heart, you read my critique of it with an open mind.

Let a word be stated regarding the extensive footnoting in the book. The benefit of sourcing these materials is that the reader will understand that I am not constructing some "straw man" with which to argue. The persons referred to are real persons who have written or spoken words communicating real ideas. In referencing both the sources and the Scriptures, I have attempted to follow Paul the Apostle's advice that, "In the mouth of two or three witnesses shall every word be established" (2 Corinthians 13:1b).

Again, I want to thank my life-long friend Pastor Robert C. Gifford of Sovereign Grace Baptist Church in Dale City, Virginia, for his helpful insights and encouragement while writing these materials. I thank Margie, my wife of over forty years, for putting up with the early mornings and evenings I spent reading, studying, thinking about, and then trying to coherently write down my thoughts about the New Spirituality. Warren Smith's counsel is appreciated for drawing my attention to many resources that are referred to in this book, especially in the essay, *From Cosmos, to Chaos, to Consciousness*. I have also grown to appreciate the Discernment Group for which I write, especially Sarah Leslie and Jewel Grewe who encouraged me to put these several writings, which before were posted on the *Herescope* website, into book form. The Discernment Group also thanks Bill Howison for designing the book's cover, and David Moeller, a member of Franklin Road Baptist Church, for its printing which makes it available for any concerned to discern.

Last but not least, I thank the Spirit of Christ for the anointing by which all God's children should differentiate truth from error (1 John 4:6). This endowment makes discernment our duty as we strive to remain faithful members of Jesus' Bride during this spiritually seductive age. Will He find us faithful when He returns to end this age (See Matthew 24:4-5, 11, and 24.)?

ENDNOTES

[1] Ronald S. Miller, Editor, *As Above, So Below: Paths to Spiritual Renewal in Daily Life* (Los Angeles: Jeremy P. Tarcher, Inc., 1992).

[2] James A. Herrick, *The Making of the New Spirituality, The Eclipse of the Western Religious Tradition* (Downers Grove: InterVarsity Press, 2003) 338.

[3] Ibid.

[4] Emphasis mine, Eugene H. Peterson, *The Message: The Bible in Contemporary Language* (Colorado Springs: NavPress, 2002) 1337.

[5] Glenn Alexander Magee, *Hegel and the Hermetic Tradition* (Ithaca: Cornell University Press, 2001) 13.

[6] Monism is not related to monasticism, though the mysticism of monasticism can lead to a devotee to embrace that reality is one, and that the One is divine.

[7] Emphasis mine, Eugene H. Peterson, *The Message / / Remix* (Colorado Springs: Navpress, 2003) Ephesians 004:4-6, 2127.

[8] D.A. Carson, *The Gospel According to John* (Grand Rapids: William B. Eerdmans Publishing Company, 1991) 342.

[9] Frederick Louis Godet, *Commentary on the Gospel of John*, Volume II (Grand Rapids: Zondervan Publishing House, 1881) 98. Of the difference between Jesus and the Pharisees, Westcott wrote: "He and they belonged essentially to two different regions; the spring of their life, the sphere of their thoughts, were separated from the spring and sphere of His by an infinite chasm." See B. F. Westcott, *The Gospel According to St. John* (Grand Rapids: Wm. B. Eerdmans Publishing Company, 1950) 130.

[10] "He's Got the Whole World in His Hands," Arranged by Eugene Thomas, *The Celebration Hymnal* (Dallas: Word Music / Integrity Music, 1997) 586.

[11] After being a top seller for over thirty-five weeks, as of June 22, 2009, *The Shack* still rests in second spot on the New York *Times* bestseller list in the Paperback Trade Fiction category (http:// www. nytimes.com/pages/books/bestseller/). Millions of copies of the book are in print.

CANON OR CHAOS
Scripture and Postmodern Existentialism

> For we have not followed cunningly devised fables (*cleverly invented stories*, NIV; *cleverly devised tales*, NASB; and *cleverly devised myths*, NRSV), when we made known unto you the power and coming of our Lord Jesus Christ, but were eyewitnesses of his majesty. (2 Peter 1:16, KJV)

Absent special revelation from God about God to human beings, religion is a dicey deal—a crapshoot. One person's religious experience or belief system becomes pitted against another's, and more often than not, the interplay of the multiple spiritualities lead the devoted into the signs and wonders of a religious never-never land. But this of course, is entirely acceptable to modern romanticists[1] and existentialists[2] who want to feel good about their religion now. "That's cool. All truth is God's truth. You've got your religion and I've got mine. Kum Ba Ya!" All this is confidently asserted in spite of the fact that most religions are individually exclusive of and mutually contradictory to each another. But that's no concern to post moderns inside and outside the church who are groping for a faith—any faith—that will provide existential meaning in life.

By way of contrast, Christian believers find transcendent meaning for their lives in the Word of God—in the person of the historical Jesus and the Scriptures which bear authentic witness to Him (John 5:39, 46-47; Luke 24:27). In other words, Christians do not look within or below, but they look without and above to find the purpose for their lives.[3] Their faith is not based upon subjective and existential feelings, but upon the objective truths God has spoken through and in His Word. Yet the adequacy of this way believing is being attacked and threatened.

The Sufficiency of the Scriptures

Immediately after Paul the Apostle announced that in the course of this evil age "evil men and seducers shall wax worse and worse, deceiving, and being deceived," he stated that

> All scripture *is* given by inspiration of God, and *is* profitable for doctrine, for reproof, for correction, for instruction in righteousness: That the man of God may

be perfect, thoroughly furnished unto all good works.
(2 Timothy 3:16-17, KJV)

The Scriptures, not our feelings, are the sufficient guide to what Christians should *believe* and how they should *behave*. Positively, the Scripture defines what Christians should believe (they are *profitable for doctrine*); negatively, it informs Christians what not to believe (they are *profitable . . . for correction*); negatively, the Scriptures define how Christians should not behave (they are *profitable . . . for correction*); and positively, they define how Christians are to behave (they are *profitable . . . for instruction in righteousness*). The Bible is the "profitable" Word of God, the deposit of truth God has invested with His church for safe keeping (1 Timothy 6:20-21).

The Subversion of the Scriptures

"Sola Scriptura!" was the cry of the Protestant Reformation. Yet as initially highlighted by Harold Lindsell in his book *The Battle for the Bible* (1976), the last decades have witnessed the demise of biblical authority among evangelicals to the point where today, we find ourselves living in times like those of Amos the prophet. He described there to be "a famine in the land, not a famine of bread, nor a thirst for water, but of hearing the words of the Lord" (Amos 8:11). So seeing helpless churches starving and dying for reason of the famine, today's false prophets seize the opportunity to "speak a vision of their own heart, and not out of the mouth of the Lord" (Jeremiah 23:16b). In many former evangelical pulpits, the Scriptures are no longer taught, and correspondingly, in the pews the Scriptures are no longer learned. Survey after survey reveals the abysmal state of biblical *beliefs and behavior* within the evangelical nation. Because the movement increasingly denies the profitability of Scripture, it is becoming morally and spiritually bankrupt.[4] In the wake of this development, spiritual bailouts are now being offered by false prophets and teachers who are equally bankrupt (2 Peter 2:1 ff.).

With methods (i.e., "doing" church) having replaced the Message, the evangelical nation no longer holds the Bible to be solely sufficient in matters of faith and practice. As a result, many congregations lay dying or dead amidst the spiritual famine. Even though the life generated by the Spirit and the Word is absent among them (1 Peter 1:23), these churches like a bouquet of cut flowers continue to perpetuate "a form of godliness" even though they have separated themselves from the root of truth (2 Timothy

3:5). And that's how those who are busy "doing" church want it. Their love for the accoutrements of activities and the excitements of entertainment supersede their love for God (2 Timothy 3:4). Church is all about "them," not Him!

Impractical to Irrelevant

Having been viewed as *impractical* by the previous generation of "contemporary" Christians—too much pie in-the-sky-bye-and-bye—the Gospel is now viewed as *irrelevant* by the "emerging" church. Some of the movement's leaders profess they don't know whether the church has ever gotten the Gospel right (Compare Acts 20:21; 1 Corinthians 15:3-4.). While for the contemporaries heaven can wait, for emergents utopia cannot. They want the kingdom now.

The Substitutions for the Scriptures

So amidst all the "excitements" and "entertainments," the Bible has come to be viewed as a tired old book constantly needing *updating* with new prophecies,[5] *clarifying* by previously-lost-but-now-found Gnostic Gospels,[6] and *illuminating* from other "sacred writings," including those belonging to the world's other religions (i.e., all truth is God's truth).[7] Scriptural authority has been undermined. The Canon is in chaos. The foundation of faith set by the Savior and the Scriptures is crumbling (See 1 Corinthians 3:11; 1 Peter 2:6-7; Ephesians 2:20; Psalm 11:3.). It is no wonder that strange doctrines like "men are gods," "name-it-claim-it," and the "health and prosperity gospel" are entrenched in the consciousness of many. It matters not that such teachings directly contradict Holy Scripture. People believe the heresies anyway (2 Peter 2:1). It is no wonder that evangelicals and Roman Catholics are seeking common ground "together." The Protestant Reformation appears finished. It is no wonder that increasingly evangelicals are toying around with the mystical spiritualities of eastern religions.

But Hope Still Gropes

With the Canon of the sixty-six books of the Protestant Bible under attack, the chaos of spiritual anarchy is settling in. By deserting the Canon—the rule of faith contained in the Old and New Testament books that Jesus, Peter, and Paul authorized (See Luke 24:44-45; Matthew 16:19; 2 Peter 3:15-16.)—evangelicals have ripened themselves for deception by false teachers who, like buzzards flying overhead, are looking for an opportunity to peck at and feed upon the carnage below. Yet for many of the dying or dead, hope persists that some new book, any book, will provide them with a magical mystical cure, explain the mystery of God's ways in a novel, exciting and entertaining way and will reveal grand new vistas of spirituality to them.

The Insufficiency of the Scriptures

In this context, Wm. Paul Young's book *The Shack*, has received rave reviews and accolades from readers, some of whom have read the spiritual allegory several times. Eugene Peterson stated that, "This book has the potential to do for our generation what John Bunyan's *Pilgrim's Progress* did for his. It's that good!"[8] Other notable endorsers say, "*The Shack* will leave you craving for the presence of God . . . The story reads like a prayer . . . *The Shack* is spiritually profound," and so on.[9]

With Bible study groups forming around *The Shack* (Now there's an oxymoron—a "Bible" study group studying *The Shack*!); is the religious allegory becoming yet another substitute for Holy Scripture? Looks like it, and the substitution may be accounted for in part because in his story Paul Young taps into the bored-and-restless skepticism resident among contemporary Christians who deny the finality of biblical authority. Cleverly, he downplays the authority and sufficiency of Scripture.

Does God Send People "Notes"?

Immediate to the plot of *The Shack* is a personal note that the main character, Mack, receives from *Papa*, or God. The note reads (*The Shack*, 16):

```
Mackenzie,
It's been a while. I've missed you.
I'll  be  back  at  the  shack  next
weekend if you
want to get together.
-Papa
```

Beginning with the note, the author's view of the Bible becomes evident: God offers troubled souls more "personal" communication than exists in Holy Scripture.

Conversations with God

On this point, we note Paul Young's accounting for the origin of his religious allegory for reason of personal and private conversations he had with God on his daily work-commute from

Gresham to Portland, Oregon. *World* magazine reports that, "Young used 80 minutes each day . . . to fill yellow legal pads with imagined conversations with God focused on suffering, pain, and evil."[10] The reporter calls the conversations "imagined." However, a friend of Young's testifies that the conversations were authentic:

> I know the author well—a personal friend. (Our whole house church devoured it last summer, and Paul came to our home to discuss it—WONDERFUL time!) The conversations that "Mack" has with God are real conversations that Paul Young had with God . . . and they revolutionized him, his family, and friends . . . When he was a broken mess, God began to speak to him. He wrote the story (rather than a "sermon") to give the real conversations context—because Jesus also used simple stories to engage our hearts, even by-passing our objecting brains, in order to have His message take root in our hearts, and grow.[11]

So where did these conversations originate? Were they real? Did they arise for reason of "notes" Young was receiving from God? Were they communications from God or his imaginations about God? Either way, "the source" is suspicious.

But to make his source credible, the author, in existentialist fashion, demeans Scripture because for existentialists, the Word is a "troublesome obstacle [that gets] . . . in the way of *the decisive conversation* between the I and the Thou."[12] For as was asked, "How can I meet a Thou if he has the written Word in between?"[13]

Vain Imaginings

The Bible does have something to say about human imagination, and it's not always good, especially if the imaginings become a "makeover" for God. In his description of idolatry, the apostle Paul places "imagination" to be the initial step into idolatry. He wrote that because they didn't know God, the heathen "glorified *him* not as God, neither were thankful; but became vain in *their imaginations*, and their foolish heart was darkened" (Emphasis mine, Romans 1:21, KJV). The word "imagination" (Greek, *dialogismos*) literally means, "the thinking of a man deliberating with himself."[14] Other versions translate imagination by "speculations" (NASB), "thinking" (NIV, NRSV), and "thoughts" (NKJV). The *New Living Translation* communicates:

> Yes . . . they began to think up foolish ideas of what God was like. The result was that their minds became dark and confused. (Romans 1:21, NLT)

Note: The Apostle states that idolatry germinates out of people "deliberating" within themselves. Is it not a foolish idea that as pictured in *The Shack*, the Father (i.e., "Papa") is hermaphroditically presented as a large African woman?

Derisive and Derogatory

To help certify the note as authentic, the author ridicules the Bible in the following scene:

> Try as he might, Mack could not escape the desperate possibility that the note just might be from God after all, even if the thought of God passing notes did not fit well with his theological training. In seminary he had been taught that God had completely stopped any overt communication with moderns, preferring to have them only listen to and follow sacred Scripture, properly interpreted, of course. God's voice had been reduced to paper, and even that paper had to be moderated and deciphered by the proper authorities and intellects. It seemed that direct communication with God was something exclusively for the ancients and uncivilized . . . Nobody wanted God in a box, just in a book. Especially an expensive one bound in leather with gilt edges, or was it guilt edges? (*The Shack*, 65-66)

Again, via musings of his main character, the author takes another jab at Scripture. "To his amusement" the story reads, Mack "also found a Gideon's Bible in the nightstand." (*The Shack*, 115)

Young's *derogatory swipe* at Holy Scripture (that people prefer God in book, especially an expensive leather one with "guilt edges") is self-indicting. He too puts God in a book—his book! He too has put God's voice on paper—his paper! The only question for seekers after truth is: whose paper are they going to believe, Young's or God's?

Regarding his *derisive swipe* against Holy Scripture (that Mack found his discovery of a Gideon Bible to be "quaintly funny"), I would point to personal testimonies of those who, finding themselves in desperate straits, found comfort from reading a Gideon Bible they found in the hotel room where they were staying.

The Canon: Open or Closed?

Does God still send people personal notes? Is the Canon closed? Any validity for the allegory hangs upon the answers to these questions. Though "narrow minded" Christians may want to keep God in a book, *The Shack's* author appears to keeping his revelatory options open. Because God still sends notes, Young infers that prophecies are ongoing, and that people can still receive written communications from God. The allegory presents the Scriptures to be insufficient in matters of faith, and as someone once said, "All heresy is either the Bible *plus*, or the Bible *minus*." In this vein, we note that *The Shack* adds "notably" to and subtracts "derisively" from the Word of God. We turn to the question of whether or not the Canon is open, or closed?

Mormons believe it's open. From off gold tablets supposedly guarded by the angel *Moroni*, their prophet Joseph Smith (1805-1844) translated revelations from God that comprise the *Book of Mormon*. Given the worldwide rise of Mormonism, it can be seen that the question regarding a closed Canon is not inconsequential. Can a legitimate case be constructed from Scripture that limits the operation of the prophetic gift to within the apostolic age? Should God's written communication be restricted to the apostolic books that through the centuries a majority consensus within the Protestant church has accorded the status of Holy Scripture?

Prophecies and "The Perfect"

The apostle Paul did state, "If *there are gifts of* prophecy, they will be done away" (1 Corinthians 13:8, NASB). The question is not *whether* prophecies will be done away with—they will—but only *when*, and that would happen when "the perfect comes," for Paul wrote: "For we know in part, and we prophesy in part; but when the perfect comes, the partial will be done away" (1 Corinthians 13:9-10). So to what does "the perfect" refer? Upon this question's answer hangs the issue as to whether people are still getting "notes" or having "conversations" with God, thereby leaving the impression that the Word of God cannot be restricted to the Bible, and that the revelatory process remains open and ongoing. So is the Christian faith, which is measured and regulated by the books comprising the Canon, fixed or in flux? As regards the rule of faith in the church, the issue looms huge.

Much depends upon the meaning of the phrase "when the perfect comes" (Greek, οταν δε ελθη το τελειον), especially the identification of "the perfect." Generally, those advocating the *continuation* of the prophetic gift interpret "the perfect" to refer to Christ and His Second Coming. Those who approximate a *cessation* of the prophetic gift at the closing of the apostolic age, interpret "the perfect" to refer to the era during which the church matured. A grown-up church no longer needed the prophetic gift!

"Perfect" and the Parousia

For a number of reasons, the interpretation that "the perfect" refers to Jesus' Second Coming is the least probable. *First*, Jesus and the apostles employed a technical word to refer to His Second Coming, the Greek word *parousia*, meaning "presence." Paul knew the word and frequently used it (1 Corinthians 15:23; 1 Thessalonians 2:19; 3:13; 4:15; 5:23; 2 Thessalonians 2:1, 8, 9). Can it not be assumed that if the apostle meant to equate "the perfect" with Jesus' Second Coming he would have employed the technical word for it? Though *parousia* was part of his vocabulary, he did not.

"Perfect" and the Personal

Second, the substantive "the perfect" (το τελειον) is neuter. Had Paul meant "the perfect" to Jesus Christ, would he not have used a masculine form of the adjective *teleios*?

For these and other reasons, I believe "the perfect" refers to the spiritual maturation process that the early church underwent from the time of its Pentecostal birth (See 1 Corinthians 2:6; 14:20; Ephesians 4:13; Colossians 1:28; 4:12.). Confirming this understanding in the following verse, Paul testifies that, "When I was a child, I used to speak as a child, think as a child, reason as a child; when I became a man, I did away with childish things" (1 Corinthians 13:11).

"The Faith": Fixed and Final

Third, in the apostolic era Jude appealed to Christian believers to, "contend earnestly for *the faith* which was *once for all delivered* to the saints" (Emphasis mine, Jude 3, NASB). In the New Testament the word for faith (Greek, *pistis*) can refer to either *the dependence of trust* (believing on the Lord Jesus Christ), or *the deposit of truth* (the Christian Gospel and the doctrines which attend it). The latter is the sense of Jude's appeal (Compare Galatians 1:22-23.). Believers are to contend for the faith once deposited.[15]

Because "the faith" was "once delivered" (Greek, *hapax*) to the saints, it will not change and cannot be altered.[16] The faith possesses fixed boundaries. The faith is not emerging. Though the working of the faith is dynamic—the Word changes people's lives—faith's content is static. Because the boundaries of it are fixed, Christians are to contend for the faith (excruciating exertion is implied). They are to do so because, "certain persons have crept in unnoticed, those who were long beforehand marked out for this condemnation, ungodly persons who turn the grace of our God into licentiousness and deny our only Master and Lord, Jesus Christ" (Jude 4).

"I think I'll write the Bible!"

Fourth, the Scriptures did not originate with man. Peter explained, "But know this first of all, that no prophecy of Scripture is *a matter* of one's own interpretation, for no prophecy was ever made by an act of human will, but men moved by the Holy Spirit spoke from God" (2 Peter 1:19-20, NASB).

In this verse, we note the phrase, "one's own interpretation." I would argue that what Peter meant does not concern the interpretation of the Scriptures, but rather the origination of the Scriptures. The follow-up and explanatory expression—"no prophecy was ever made by an act of human will"—argues to the point. In other words, someone did not sit down one day and say, "I think I'll write the Bible!" No. Scripture is of uncommon, not common derivation. It originated from holy men who were moved by the Holy Spirit.

Lewis Sperry Chafer, the founder of Dallas Theological Seminary, once stated, "The Bible is not such a book that man would write if he could, or could write if he would." Think about it . . . in the world of comparative religions, all alone, New Covenant Christianity teaches that salvation comes to us as a gift of God. All other of the world's religions tell us that by some means we must earn it. Yet we are saved by God's unmerited favor, by His grace!

God's Last Word in these Last Days

Fifth, the finality of God's speaking to humanity is to be found in Christ. As the author of Hebrews wrote, "God, after He spoke long ago to the fathers in the prophets in many portions and in many ways, in these last days has spoken to us in *His* Son . . ." (Hebrews 1:1-2). Christian apologist and theologian Cornelius Van Til (1895-1987) put it like this: "Fundamental to everything orthodox is the presupposition of the antecedent self-existence of God and his infallible revelation of himself to man in the Bible."[17]

On this point there may be concern in the minds of some that *The Shack* is emerging to become a 67th book of the Protestant Canon. Increasingly, study groups, having laid their Bibles aside, have chosen *The Shack* as their study text.

Barbarians at the Gate

Existentialism attempts to separate God from anything fixed and final. They are quite comfortable dividing "what they call Christ from Jesus, from the Church, from Scripture, and from the sacraments."[18] In this regard, we note how in the allegory *Jesus* is separated from Christ. Not once is he called Christ. He's only a carpenter. We note too the story's disdain for the authority and organization of the church. Mack labels it "cloistered spirituality," and remarks that churches are "little religious social clubs" that don't "seem to make any real difference or affect any real changes." (*The Shack*, 66) And as has been pointed out in this essay, the novel deprecates Holy Scripture—"Nobody wanted God in a box, just in a book. Especially an expensive one bound in leather with gilt edges, or was it guilt edges?" (*The Shack*, 66)

Two decades ago, theologian Carl Henry discerned of trends being evidenced within the evangelical movement, that:

> Our generation is lost to the truth of God, to the reality of divine revelation, to the content of God's will, to the power of His redemption, and to the authority of His Word. For this loss it is paying dearly in a swift relapse to paganism. The savages are stirring again; you can hear them rumbling and rustling in the tempo of our times.[19]

Spiritual chaos is now consuming the Canon as the smiles of the froward spiritualities seduce naïve and unsuspecting Christians (See Proverbs 7:1-27.).

ENDNOTES

[1] Romanticism is a philosophical "reaction against the stiff rationality of the Enlightenment [e.g., its Newtonian worldview] . . . in favour of the spontaneous, the unfettered, the subjective, the imaginative and emotional, and the inspirational and heroic." See Simon Blackburn, "Romanticism, "*Oxford Dictionary of Philosophy* (New York: Oxford University Press, 2005) 320.

[2] Existentialism derives from the word "existence." The common themes of the philosophy are: "the individual, the experience of choice, and the absence of rational understanding of the universe with a consequent dread or sense of absurdity in human life." See Blackburn, "existentialism," *Dictionary of Philosophy*, 125. In my view, *The Shack's* author cleverly plays around with, in addition to other spiritualities, an integrated version of a romanticist-existentialist philosophy.

[3] "The Larger Catechism" of *The Westminster Confession of Faith* (AD 1648) begins by asking: "What is the chief and highest end of man?" and then answers, "Man's chief and highest end is to glorify God, and fully enjoy him forever."

[4] See David Kinnaman and Gabe Lyons, *Unchristian, What a New Generation Really Thinks about Christianity . . . and Why It Matters* (Grand Rapids: Baker Books, 2007) 46-48.

[5] Though admittedly anecdotal, I heard of one church where a parishioner stood and spoke a word from the Lord to the congregation. The church's sound man recorded the prophecy. During the intervening week, the church's secretary steno graphed the "prophetic" word, and the next Sunday it was read from the church's pulpit as scripture! Some may laugh . . . But why not? It's a word from God, isn't it?

[6] In the last years, especially since the publication of Dan Brown's *The Da Vinci Code* (2003), a spate of books, both attacking and defending the accuracy of the Four Gospels against Gnostic writings like *The Gospel of Thomas*, have been published. Concern about the four New Testament Gospels is widespread in both culture and church.

[7] In what is popularly known as the spiritual formation movement, *lectio divina* (Latin, "reading sacred things") is a very Roman Catholic way of slowly, deliberately, and repetitively reading sacred writings. Though the "sacred writings" include the Holy Scripture, the technique may also applied to reading other scriptures such as the *Bhagavad-Gita*, the *Torah*, or the *Koran*, and presumably any other writings possessing a sacred aura about them. Again, the Holy Scriptures are considered insufficient.

[8] William P. Young, *The Shack* (Los Angeles: Windblown Media, 2007) Front Cover.

[9] Ibid. Back Cover and Front Matter.

[10] Susan Olasky, "Commuter-driven bestseller," *World*, June 28/July 5, 2008, 49.

[11] Dena Brehm, on the interactive blog, *Christian Universalism-The Beautiful Heresy: The Shack*, posted February 14, 2008 at 11:44AM, (http://christian-universalism.blogs.com/thebeautiful heresy/2008/02/the-shack.html). Though no longer available on the blog, the author possesses a copy of the letter.

[12] Emphasis mine, Robert P. Roth, "Existentialism and Historic Christian Faith," *A Christianity Today Reader*, Frank E. Gaebelein, Editor (New York: Meredith Press, 1966) 231.

[13] Ibid.

[14] John Henry Thayer, "dialogismos," *Greek-English Lexicon of the New Testament* (Grand Rapids: Zondervan Publishing House, 1975 Reprint) 139.

[15] See Richard J. Bauckham, *Jude, 2 Peter* (Waco: Word Books, 1983) 32-33.

[16] The phrase "the faith once delivered to the saints" (Greek, τη απαξ παραδοθειση τοι αγιοις πιστει) may literally be translated, "*the* once delivered to the saints *faith*." The verb "once delivered" occurs in the passive voice (the saints received it) and in the aorist tense (the action is complete). Fanning labeled the tense's aspect, "Snapshot." In other words, faith's picture has been taken. It is what it is. The aorist here appears to be "consummative," meaning the "the cessation of an act or state." See Daniel B. Wallace, *Greek Grammar Beyond the Basics* (Grand Rapids: Zondervan Publishing House, 1996) 554, 559-561.

Yet for consumption by moderns, *The Shack's* author and approving readers presume the portrait of the faith needs to be "touched-up." But if they have read the allegory, Bible believers are left scratching their heads and asking, "How does Young's *Papa-Elousia* even begin to resemble God's self-portrait, by His words and works, in the Bible?"

[17] Cornelius Van Til, *An Introduction to Systematic Theology* (Class Syllabus, Westminster Theological Seminary, Philadelphia, 1970) 1, quoted by Clark H. Pinnock, *Tracking the Maze, Finding Our Way through Modern Theology from an Evangelical Perspective* (San Francisco: Harper & Row Publishers, 1990) 44.

[18] Roth, "Existentialism," 231.

[19] Carl F.H. Henry, *Twilight of a Great Civilization* (Westchester, Illinois: Crossway Books, 1988) 7.

THE HOLY GOD
Immanence to Idolatry

> To whom then will ye liken God? or what likeness
> will ye compare unto him? (Isaiah 40:18, KJV)

In the Old City of Jerusalem, I stood reverently before the massive stones that comprise the foundation of the mount upon which the Jewish temple once stood. Standing before the Western, or Wailing, Wall, I noticed little slips of paper tucked in the crevices between the giant hand-hewn rocks. Wondering what the papers were, I reached in with my fingers and pulled a slip out. The handwriting on the paper began "G-d." I later found out that devout Jews hold the name of God, or the Lord, so sacred that they, out of respect for Him, refuse to spell His name in a profane (i.e., common) way. Omitting the letter "o," they write "G-d" or "L-rd." I fear that, within the pale of "contemporary" Christendom, such respect, or reverence, for God has been, or is being, lost. God has become "cuddly-common" to us. In this spirit, we turn to address the subject of God's nearness, or immanence.

God's immanence is opposite to His transcendence. Both of these categories of thought about God attempt to describe His relationship to His universe—to nature, to nations, to people, to the animal kingdom, and so on. Theologians employ the terms to describe both God's involvement with (immanence) and separation from (transcendence) His created cosmos. The Bible pictures God as being both near and far from His creation. He is immanently near us, but He is also transcendently apart from us.

While God is not spatial but Spirit (John 4:24), the Word describes Him as being both above and below. To our thinking, these opposites should to remain in tension to each other. To view God as transcendently distant leads to Deism (i.e., God created, but is not actively involved in the world.). To view God as immanently near leads to Pantheism[1] (Creation is god.) or Panentheism (God permeates creation, and as such, nature contains God.). As one young blogger expresses it, "We need, somehow, to have God in our world without our world containing God. We need, somehow, God outside our world without eliminating him from it . . . If God is in our world then he's less than God, if outside it, He's irrelevant."[2]

As with His transcendence, speculation about God's immanence is born out of philosophical theology. Erickson acknowledges that, "The doctrine of divine immanence was not prominent in much of the history of Christian thought."[3] The word "providence" therefore becomes a better description of God's relationship to creation. Immanence denotes a divine being in creation. Providence denotes divine sovereignty over creation. After acknowledging biblical passages demonstrating God's operation in the world (Genesis 34:14-15; Acts 17:27-28; Psalm 135:7; Matthew 5:45; 10:29-30; Colossians 1:16-17; etc.), Erickson admits, "It is significant to note that the texts that we cited as evidence of God's immanence primarily refer to his action, his activity."[4] In other words, God's providence over creation, rather than His presence in, around, and through nature, better describes God's relationship to the world. This may appear to be quibbling over words, but given the state of today's spirituality, it is not.

Pantheistic New Age religion fondly speaks of God as vibrating immanence, energy, or the Force. In a quantum way, this god moves unpredictably in atoms, plants, people, and more. Over the past fifty years this brand of spirituality has been influencing American spirituality, and appears to be emerging in the evangelical church. God as immanent seems to be eclipsing God as transcendent. By their emphasis in one text of Scripture upon the God's being immanent, some Bible versions sacrifice the attribute of God's holiness.

The *New Century Version* states, "There is one God and Father of everything. He rules everything and is everywhere *and is in everything*" (Emphasis mine, Ephesians 4:6, NCV).[5] Taking the last clause (*God . . . is in everything*) at face value, should we not think it clearly states that God is "in" everything? If so, then this Bible version promotes pantheism, and pantheism contradicts the biblical teaching that the Holy God is separate from His creation.

God's dominant attribute in the Old Testament is His holiness, or separateness from His creation.[6] The Psalmist wrote:

> The Lord is great in Zion; and he is high above all the people. Let them praise thy great and terrible name; for it is holy. . . . Exalt ye the Lord our God, and worship at his footstool; for he is holy. . . . Exalt the Lord our God . . . for the Lord our God is holy" (Psalm 99:3, 5, 9; Compare Isaiah 6:3; 55:8-9; Revelation 4:8; etc.).

But what exactly is God's holiness? Likely, the Old Testament word for "holy" (Hebrew, *qds*) derives from a root meaning to "to cut or separate." As regards God being holy, one Old Testament scholar observed:

> The basic idea conveyed by the holiness of God is His separateness . . . the One who stands apart from and above the creation. . . . It is no exaggeration to state that this element overshadows all others in the character of the deity . . .[7]

If not separate and distinct from His creation, then God is not holy. Based upon holiness' essential meaning, how can it be thought that, as the NCV reads, "God . . . is in everything"? If God is "in" everything then He is not holy, and this New Age idea of God is the spawning bed for idolatry (See Isaiah 40:18-25.).

For reason of its pantheistic implications, immanency, if unrestrained, leads to idolatry, for pantheism (i.e., nature worship) is idolatry. It's worshipping the creation rather than the Creator (See Romans 1:21-23.). But Hannah exalted God praying, "There is no one holy like the Lord, / Indeed, there is no one besides Thee, / *nor is there any rock like our God*" (Emphasis mine, 2 Samuel 2:20, NASB). In light of the fact that the Bible presents God as "Holy Other," the trend of contemporary Bible versions to flirt with the New Age belief that nature is (pantheism) or contains (panentheism) divinity—god even being in rocks—is concerning.

For example, in his book *The Purpose Driven Life*, Pastor Rick Warren quotes the NCV of Ephesians chapter four and verse six. He prefaces his quotation with the statement that, "God is with you all the time. No place is any closer to God than the place where you are right now."[8] His citation of the verse and his comments reflect insensitivity to the influence of New Age religion upon American culture.

A Rick Warren defender argues that Warren did not say everything is divine. True. He did not say it, but the Bible version he quotes *in*ferences it. About God, the NCV plainly states, "He . . . is in everything." But Warren, says Richard Abanes, meant to teach God's immanence which he associates with God's omnipresence. He writes: "The thrust of the passage is God's presence not only above and beyond the universe, but also throughout it (His omnipresence)."[9]

Abanes' defense of Warren on this point is confusing. The last two clauses of the NCV read that God "is everywhere *and is in everything*" (Emphasis mine, Ephesians 4:6). In that, according to Abanes, the first clause teaches God's omnipresence/immanence, how then should we understand the second clause? Does it possess the same theological implication as the preceding clause? I don't think so. If the referent of omnipresence/immanence is the first clause, "God . . . is everywhere," then how can the second clause, "God . . . is in everything," again be interpreted to mean "God is everywhere"? Such an interpretation makes the two clauses redundant. If the first clause is understood to refer to God's omnipresence/immanence, the only "natural" meaning for the second clause, "is in everything," is panentheistic or pantheistic.

Similarly, "self-esteem" preacher Robert H. Schuller believes that God is immanent in humanity. And if that is the case, Erickson notes God must necessarily be "immanent within all persons in the same sense."[10] So Schuller boldly announced, "Yes, God is alive and He is in every single human being!"[11] To him, God is within all people, and this he advocates despite the fact that Scripture teaches the opposite (See Romans 8:9 and John 8:44.). Apparently, this is where the "self-esteem gospel" leads. There remains but one more "baby step" for Schuller and his followers to take—the step from self-esteem to self-worship.

Believing in God's immanence carries certain implications. Over the last two centuries, one theologian notes that the understanding of God has trended toward immanency.[12] To account for this trend, he offers six reasons: 1. Contact and interaction between the world's cultures encourages religious pluralism; 2. Psychologizing life eliminates sin as a barrier between God and man; 3. Quantum physics has revolutionized how the cosmos is perceived (i.e., no longer "above-below" and "up-down" categories of thought); 4. Monistic-pantheistic New Age religion eliminates belief in God's transcendence (i.e., God is one of us); 5. Casual relationships have replaced formal ones; and, 6. The entertainment industry consistently profanes God by making Him out to be a man (or woman?). All these factors contribute to the modern viewing of God to be more immanent than transcendent. Furthermore, *The Shack* evidences all six of these theological trends.

But ideas have consequences, and never more so than with the ideas men have about God. Immanentism makes special revelation from God unnecessary. Revelation is reduced to "consciousness or conversational insight." As such, all literature, even *The Shack*, manifests some inspiration. Immanentism also makes Jesus' incarnation unnecessary. Every human birth is a "miracle." The difference between humanity and Christ becomes one of degree, not kind. All possess the Christ spirit and the potential, like Mack in *The Shack*, to develop it. Immanentism also makes atonement unnecessary, especially a penal substitutionary atonement.[13] For reason of His permeating immanent love, no separation between God and humanity exists. Sin becomes an illusory barrier that developing new consciousness will solve. Because salvation is believed to come from below and not from above, the Gospel morphs to become a social gospel.

Additionally, immanentism blurs distinction between moral right and wrong. After citing how German Christians embraced Adolf Hitler on the assumption that whatever happened in history was God's will, Erickson observes the danger that, "If God is totally immanent within the creation and history, there is no outside objective standard for making ethical evaluations."[14]

Finally, immanentism makes prayer unnecessary. God is already involved in the processes of life. Therefore, in the latter part of his life Paul Tillich admitted he no longer prayed. He only meditated.

But the God who is worthy of our praise and prayers is the One who is provident and "Holy Other." That's why in heaven the four creatures continually praise Him, "Holy, holy, holy, Lord God Almighty, which was, and is, and is to come" (Revelation 4:8, KJV).

ENDNOTES

[1] The best way to understand Pantheism is by contrasting it to Theism: Theism—God minus the universe equals God! Pantheism—God minus the universe equals nothing! In Pantheism God and creation are identical. Pan*en*theism offers a slightly different twist: Creation serves as God's container. In both systems of thought, God is "wholly immanent."

[2] Daniel Silliman, "The Wholly Other and the Possibility of a Theological Language" (http:// www. sillimandoc.blogspot.com /2005_09_01_sillimandoc_archive.html#112768601263660448).

[3] Millard J. Erickson, *God the Father Almighty, A Contemporary Exploration of the Divine Attributes* (Grand Rapids: Baker Books, 1998) 263.

[4] Ibid. 271.

[5] Compare Eugene H. Peterson, *The Message // Remix* (Colorado Springs: Navpress, 2003) 2127. "You have . . . one God and Father of all, who . . . is present in all. *Everything* you are and think and do *is permeated with Oneness*" (Emphasis mine, Ephesians 004:6). *Today's English Version* also reads that, "there is one God and Father of all mankind, who is Lord of all [mankind?], works through all [mankind?], and is in all [mankind?]" (My bracketed questions, Ephesians 4:6).

[6] God's holiness is both essential and ethical (1 Peter 1:14-16). Profane beliefs about God induce profane behavior before God. Immorality issues from idolatry, and idolatry happens when people lose sight of God's holiness portrayed in Scripture (See Leviticus 19:1-4.).

[7] E.F. Harrison, "Holiness; Holy," *The International Standard Bible Encyclopedia*, Geoffrey W. Bromiley, General Editor, Volume 2 (Grand Rapids: William B. Eerdmans Publishing Company, 1982) 725. As another scholar summarizes, "God's holiness thus becomes an expression for his perfection of being that transcends everything creaturely." See Jackie A. Naudé, "7727 קדשׁ" *New International Dictionary of Old Testament Theology & Exegesis*, Volume 3, Willem A. VanGemeren, General Editor (Grand Rapids: Zondervan Publishing House, 1997) 879.

[8] Rick Warren, *The Purpose Driven Life* (Grand Rapids: Zondervan, 2002) 88.

[9] See Richard Abanes, *Rick Warren and the Purpose that Drives Him* (Eugene, Oregon: Harvest House Publishers, 2005) 95. My exegesis of Ephesians 4:6 interprets the verse as follows: Paul affirms God's presence in and lordship over the church. Though God is omnipresent in the cosmos (Psalm 139:7), Paul was not stating that in the last clause. He is teaching that God is particularly present in the universal church.

[10] Robert H. Schuller, "Hour of Power," Program #1762, p. 5, cited by Warren Smith, *Deceived On Purpose, The New Age Implications of the Purpose-Driven Church*, Second Edition (Magalia, California: Mountain Stream Press, 2004) 80-81.

[11] Millard J. Erickson, *Christian Theology*, Second Edition (Grand Rapids: Baker Books, 1998) 333.

[12] Erickson, *God the Father*, 260-261.

[13] *More Books and Things . . .* , March 11, 2009, Transcript of Interview on Radio Station KAYP (http:// morebooksandthings. blogspot.com/2009/03/transcript-of-interview.html). In this interview, Young denies the penal substitutionary atonement.

[14] Erickson, *Christian Theology*, 336.

ELOUSIA AND THE BLACK MADONNA
Imagination, Images, and Impurity in "The Shack"[1]

> To whom will ye liken me, and make *me* equal, and
> compare me that we may be like? . . . Remember
> the former things of old: for I *am* God, and *there is*
> none else; *I am* God, and *there is* none like me . . .
> (Isaiah 46:5, 9, KJV)

God is Truth. That He is Truth distinguishes Him from
idols which are false.[2] To the Thessalonians Paul remarked how
they "turned to God from idols to serve a living and true God" (1
Thessalonians 1:9, NASB). Of the Lord, the prophet declared,
"There is none like Thee, O Lord; Thou art great, and great is Thy
name in might." He then explained regarding those who create
idols: "But they are altogether stupid and foolish in their discipline
of delusion—their idol is wood!" The prophet then commented:

> Beaten silver is brought from Tarshish, and gold from
> Uphaz, the work of a craftsman and of the hands of a
> goldsmith; violet and purple are their clothing; they are
> all the work of skilled men. But the Lord is the true
> God . . . (Jeremiah 10:6, 8-10, NASB).

In this vein, A.W. Tozer once wrote: "What comes into our minds
when we think about God is the most important thing about us."[3]

But idols arise from human imagination. Humans can
design God however they want him, her, them, or it to be. In his
description of the descent into idolatry, the Apostle Paul wrote:

> Because that, when they knew God, they glorified him
> not as God, neither were thankful; but became vain in
> their *imaginations*, and their foolish heart was darkened.
> Professing themselves to be wise, they became fools,
> and changed the glory of the incorruptible God into an
> *image* made like to corruptible man" (Emphasis mine,
> Romans 1:21-23a, KJV).

Imagination creates images—even idolatrous images—and the
images can either be material or mental, visual or verbal.

Someone once said that a picture is worth a thousand
words. In an image-oriented age where people watch more and

read less, the statement makes its point. But words can also create images, powerful images. Through the mind's eye, we see. So the question arises, in his bestselling novel *The Shack*, what image of God is Wm. Paul Young painting with the strokes of his verbal brush? I am fearful that the book's imaginative picture of God, even though fictional, presents the wrong image of Him.

But to understand the book's covert message, we need to look at the overt picture of God drawn by the author. As we do, we would ask the question, from whence might the author have derived the concept of his goddess? As we proceed, we shall look at pieces of evidence to see if between goddess religion and "Papa-Elousia," the first member of the polymorphous trinity in *The Shack*, there exist any resemblance. We shall attempt to connect the dots, to discover where the author's picture of God might be "sourced," and then seeing how *The Shack's* composite picture of deity *is* linked to "goddess-ism," we will address the potential implications of such theology for those who might seek to cultivate a spiritual relationship with the feminine-divine. In developing the implication of goddess-ism's invasion into Christianity, we will begin by employing the Apostle Paul's paradigmatic description of idolatry in Romans 1:19-32. Generally, he describes the deconstruction of God to occur in three phases.

PHASE ONE: *Imagination*

Let the obvious be stated at the outset: *The Shack* is a work of fiction, a work of imagination. For reason of the caricature of God it presents, does the "it's-only-fiction" excuse exonerate the book from the charge of heresy? I think not.

First, no book in the Protestant Bible is of the fiction genre. The Bible is not a book of make-believe. *Second*, by their very definition, idols are fictions. As the Apostle Paul warned, "For the time will come when they will not endure sound doctrine; but after their own lusts shall they heap to themselves teachers, having itching ears; and they shall turn away *their* ears from the truth, and shall be turned unto fables" (Question: might the word 'fable' be legitimately paraphrased, 'fictions'?—2 Timothy 4:3-4, KJV). *Third*, apocryphal, pseudepigraphical, and Gnostic writings are also mostly fiction, yet are venerated by many. Just because literature is categorized as fiction does not neutralize "the spirituality" people might assign to it. *Fourth*, stories often attempt to underscore and strengthen real perceptions. The story of *The Shack* may represent the manner in which the author struggled with and worked through disappointments in his life. If the explanation and solution are real to him, then we can project that they might also be real to others who have suffered devastating life experiences. And *fifth*, imagination is the spawning ground for idolatry (Romans 1:21). Ideas have consequences, and a big problem exists when people come to believe that their thoughts inform them about God's nature and character (See Isaiah 55:8-9.). Idolatry is thinking wrong thoughts about God, and words are the vehicles of thoughts. Old Testament scholar Peter Craigie remarks:

> Too easily in our modern world we forget the implications of the second of the Ten Commandments; it prohibits the construction of images of God. And although few of us are tempted to construct an image of wood or stone, too soon we construct images of words, which can constrict the conception of God as readily as the material image.[4]

So with this in mind, we proceed to look at where Young's verbal images of the goddess *Elousia* might be sourced.

PHASE TWO: *Idolatry*

Does *The Shack* construct a verbal idol? We will look at three pagan goddess images to see if they bear similarity to "Elousia," the goddess created by the author (Exodus 20:3-6).

The Black Madonna

Having finished reading *The Shack*, and while surfing the Internet, I was quite smitten when inadvertently I ran across an article written by Rev. Dr. Matthew Fox, *The Return of the Black Madonna: A Sign of Our Times or How the Black Madonna is Shaking Us Up for the Twenty-First Century.*[5] Fox's description of *The Black Madonna* (or the ancient Egyptian goddess *Isis* as she is also known) included her ability to guide distressed persons to find emotional healing within. At first glance, this description seemed to possess an eerie parallel to the black goddess character ("Elousia") created in *The Shack*. Upon further reflection, it became evident the similarity between them is more than color. Similar personas emerge in both writings. We note some resemblances between Fox's "Black Madonna" and Young's "Elousia."

First, Fox states:

> The Black Madonna invites us into the dark and
> therefore into our depths. This is what the mystics call
> the "inside" of things, the essence of things. This is
> where Divinity lies. It is where the true self lies. It is
> where illusions are broken apart and the truth lies.[6]

In *The Shack*, we note the word "darkness" occurs frequently. It is as if darkness is archetypal to Mack's *Great Sadness*. This resemblance is especially noticeable when he appears before "Sophia." In the chapter "Here Come Da Judge," darkness is the dominant aura surrounding Mack's experience. As he entered the cave, "with his hands outstretched in front of him," Young writes that "he ventured a couple of steps into the inky darkness and stopped." (*The Shack*, 151) To create Mack's experience, Young amplifies references to "darkness"—"deep shadows . . . inky blackness . . . dim light . . . darkened room." Mack dealt with his sadness by entering the darkness. But Scripture reminds us that, "God is light, and in Him is no darkness at all" (1 John 1:5, KJV).

Second, Fox also notes:

> The Black Madonna calls us to Grieve. The Black
> Madonna is the sorrowful mother, the mother who
> weeps tears for the suffering in the universe, the
> suffering in the world, the brokenness of our very
> vulnerable hearts.[7]

According to Fox, *The Black Madonna* "invites us to enter into our grief and name it and be there to learn what suffering has to teach us."[8] He writes:

> To grieve is to enter what John of the Cross in the
> sixteenth century called the 'dark night of the soul.' We
> are instructed not to run from this dark night but to
> stay there to learn what darkness has to teach us.[9]

In *The Shack*, at the climactic moment when "Papa" (a.k.a. "Elousia," the black goddess) enfolded Mack into his/her arms and gently invited him to "Let it all out," the story records that in a moment of deep emotional catharsis, Mack "closed his eyes as the tears poured out . . . He wept until he had cried out all the darkness, all the longing and all the loss, until there was nothing left." (*The Shack*, 226)

Fourth, Fox states that, "The Black Madonna calls us to our Divinity which is also our Creativity." He goes on to state that *The Black Madonna* "expects nothing less from us than creativity. Hers is a call to create, a call to ignite the imagination."[10] On the next point Fox again states:

> The Black Madonna calls us to Diversity. There is no imagination without diversity—imagination is about inviting disparate elements into soul and culture so that new combinations can make love together and new beings can be birthed."[11]

Fox's *Black Madonna* calls persons to an imaginative consciousness which has nothing to do with scriptural reality.

Likewise, when the goddess-like *Sophia* calls upon Mack to role play as *The Judge*, to sit in judgment over all other persons including God, she notes his pensiveness about assuming such an awesome responsibility. *Sophia* says to Mack: "'Your imagination,' she interrupted his train of thought, 'is not serving you well at this moment'." (*The Shack*, 160) In the Front Matter of the book, Greg Albrecht informs the potential reader, "You will be captivated by the creativity and imagination of *The Shack*, and before you know it, you'll be experiencing God as never before." Young's novel itself serves to ignite the imagination, something Fox writes that the returning Black Madonna is also doing. At the emotional level, the goddess spirituality of *The Shack* and the Black-Madonna resemble one another.

Other parallels between Fox's "Black Madonna" and *The Shack's* "Elousia"—their gender diversity, nurturing of hurting hearts, emphasis upon developing personal relationships, concern for the environment, and so on—form archetypal metaphors around which the mystery of life and suffering can be probed and explained, and upon which transcendent values can be formulated and applied for the social welfare and unity of the world's diverse and divided population. These ecumenical metaphors are increasingly becoming popular in the Emergent Church.

"Goddess PAPA"

Bearing striking similarity to Young's naming of *Papa-Elousia* in his book, there is also a goddess in the Polynesian pantheon known as, "Goddess PAPA."[12] Of this goddess it is claimed:

From Her we find comfort and Care
Of Unconditional Love in Times of Crises and Grief
Her intervention instills calming reassurance and Healing
All can call upon Goddess Papa for Guidance . . .[13]

As to name, nature, and nurturing potential, Young's feminine "Elousia" bears an uncanny similarity to the "Goddess PAPA" of Polynesian lore. It can only be surmised whether the author might have derived his concept of "Papa-Elousia" from Polynesian paganism, or places thereabouts?[14] However, there may be more evidence connecting Young's feminine-divine caricature to the feminine-divine of pagan mythology.

"The Breasted One"

The following dialog, I think, sheds additional light upon where Young's goddess-ism might be sourced. In defending his caricature of God as feminine, and as they discussed the role of anthropomorphisms in describing God, this exchange took place between a talk-show host, Matt Slick, and *The Shack's* author:

> SLICK: They [various Old Testament writers] know he [God] doesn't have a nose and nostrils.
> YOUNG: Sure, we know that he's not male or female. So every use of imagery of God as male is just as inadequate as every use of God as female. Sure, we know that.
> SLICK: Well, actually that's gonna come and get you here in a minute.
> YOUNG: So—so he is male? You have a God who is male?
> SLICK: I didn't say that. Why does God refer to himself and Jesus refer to him as Father?
> YOUNG: Well, why is he called *El Shaddai*, which is "the breasted one"?
> SLICK: Well, that's nice. But, why is he called the Father? And why is the Son [interrupt]?
> YOUNG: Because it's relational.
> SLICK: What kind of relationship?
> YOUNG: It's the relationship of Father and Son.[15]

Added to his apparent allusions to Roman Catholicism's *Black Madonna* and the Polynesian *Goddess PAPA*, the author again appears to have projected into God a quality derived from a radical-feminist perspective; namely, that *El Shaddai* means "breasted one." But where might Paul Young have derived such an idea about God? Does the meaning really reside in a name for God that's in the Bible?

The Feminist Connexion

The name "breasted one" appears to be sourced in feminist spirituality. In Part One ("The Feminine Divine in the Hebrew Scriptures") of her book, *Delighting in the Feminine Divine*, Bridget Mary Meehan, states that, "D.F. Stramara translates *El Shaddai* (a name for the Divine in the Hebrew Scripture as 'God the breasted one'.)" [16] But for several reasons, the inference that the divine name *El Shaddai* means "breasted one" is ludicrous. It is an imagined meaning pulled out of thin air.

First, *Shaddai* is a masculine noun! If it referred to a goddess, then we would expect the noun to be feminine in gender.

Second, *Shaddai* is a singular noun. If the noun meant "breasted one," then we would look for it to occur in the plural.

Third, the Hebrew name *Shaddai* is of uncertain origin.[17] Nevertheless, no standard lexical authority suggests the idea of "breasted one" being the etymological base from which this name for God is derived.

Fourth, to be constructed to even remotely resemble the meaning of "breasted one," a second letter "d" (Hebrew, dālet) needs to be added (Though *Shaddai* possesses two "d's" in the English transliteration, it possesses but one "d" (Hebrew, "dālet") in the original text (i.e., *Sha-dai*).[18]

And finally, if the meaning "the breasted one" be accepted, then might it be considered that—God forbid—Artemis-Dianna, the many breasted goddess of Ephesus, was a type of *Shaddai*? If with her many breasts Artemis is *Shaddai*–like, then Paul the Apostle needlessly stirred up controversy at Ephesus when he preached against the goddess in that ancient city (See Acts 19:23-41.). Painting God as feminine for reason of importing a foreign meaning of "the breasted one" into *Shaddai* is an irresponsible leap into the interpretive dark. Yet, by Young's own admission, that, in part, explains why he painted God to be "Papa-Elousia."

PHASE THREE: *Impurity*

After identifying *El Shaddai* as "the breasted one," Meehan becomes a "spiritual director" and recommends the following "Questions for Personal Reflection or Group Discussion":

What new insights or understandings about God do
you discover through this *image*? What *images* of God
come from your reflection on women's sexuality? How
do you feel about these *images*? What *images*, feelings,
insights express your experience of your sexuality?[19]

Set against the backdrop of this spiritual director's advice,
the Apostle's description of idolatry becomes vivid. He states:
"Professing to be wise, they became fools, and exchanged the glory
of the incorruptible God for an *image* in the form of corruptible
man [woman?] . . ." (Romans 1:22-23a). *Images . . . image*, is the
idolatrous picture continuing to emerge?

But there is a final question asked in *Delighting in the
Feminine Divine*: "How does your sexuality affect your spirituality?"[20]
At this juncture, we must note where the answer to this question
might lead. Wrote the Apostle, "Therefore God gave them over in
the lusts of their hearts to *impurity*, that their bodies might be
dishonored among them" (Emphasis mine, Romans 1:24).

Exodus and Idolatry

This whole degrading process may be tracked back to
Israel's Egyptian captivity and the subsequent post-exodus worship
of the golden calf (Ezekiel 20:7-9; Exodus 32:1-35). After their
divine deliverance from Egypt, the Israelites *imagined* they needed
"a god" to feel close to, one who was present with them, and not
some unseen and distant deity who either wouldn't or couldn't
meet their needs.[21] So in Moses' absence, they told Aaron, "Come,
make us a god who will go before us . . ." (Exodus 32:1, NASB).[22]
So under Aaron's supervision, they collected jewelry from the
women and young people that was then smelted and molded into
the *image* of a golden bull, symbolizing the power they felt was
needed to provide for and protect them in the wilderness.

But failing to "feel" the divine nearness to them (By
themselves idols can't do that.), the Israelites decided, as they did
with making the idol, to stimulate a divine presence. To raise the
excitement over the idol they had built, Aaron called for a party
(Exodus 32:5). The Scripture records the worship turned sexual as
they "rose up to play" (Exodus 32:6b; Compare 1 Corinthians 10:7-
8.). The Hebrew word for "play" (*tsachaq*) possesses a sensual
meaning as when Abimelech observed Isaac "caressing" (*tsachaq*)
Rebekah, or when Potiphar's wife accused Joseph of attempting to
make sexual "sport" (*tsachaq*) of her (See Genesis 26:8; 39:14, 17.).

The Israelites were "completely given over to their desire."[23] As to this developing situation, a commentator remarks, "The people themselves assume control . . . a religious orgy has begun."[24] Israel's *idolatry* led them to *impurity*.

Similarly, where might an imagining of the feminine-divine lead us? Remember . . . ideas have consequences. Might *The Shack* actually be painting an image of God that if embraced, could lead to a spiritual infidelity that will contribute to the demise of the relationship between people and God? Could an infusion of the feminine-divine into the collective psyche of many contemporary Christians actually stimulate, cultivate, and facilitate the entrance of sexual impurity into the church?

The Shack does contain moments of subtle sensuality. For example, upon hearing the sensual *Sophia* ask him, during a séance-like journey into the darkness, "Do you understand why you're here?" the story records:

> Mack could almost feel her words rain down on his head first and melt into his spine, sending delicious tingles everywhere. He shivered and decided that he never wanted to speak again. He only wanted her to talk . . . (*The Shack*, 153)

Or consider the moment when *Sarayu*, in affirming her constant presence with Mack, told him, "I am always with you; sometimes I want you to be aware in a special way—more intentional." Then Young records that Mack, "distinctly felt her presence in the tingle down his spine." (*The Shack*, 195)

We now proceed to look at the theology of *The Shack*.[25] We turn to the ideas presented in the book about God. The god of *The Shack* (As to His divine name, I refuse to spell God with an upper case "G.") is an imagined hermaphroditic and polymorphic trinity, consisting of a retreat-center owner and hostess who goes by the name of *Elousia*, a carpenter-handyman named *Jesus*, and a gardener identified by the name of *Sarayu*. In order, we consider the three members of this polymorphous trinity along with another omniscient and sensual lady who in *The Shack* goes by the name of *Sophia*, or Wisdom.

The First Person

At first mention, and according to Mack's wife Nan's understanding, the first person of the godhead goes by the name of

Papa (perhaps alluding to the Apostle Paul's designation of Him as "Abba," Romans 8:15). But upon Mack's arrival at the shack, *Papa* morphs into a large and loving African-American woman named *Elousia* (i.e., a combination of the Hebrew name for God the Creator, "El," and the Greek word "ousia" suggesting the Platonic meaning of "being" or "existence").[26] Among other characteristics, *Elousia* describes herself as, "the Creator God who is truly real and the ground of all being."(*The Shack*, 111)

Ground of Being

This description of God appears to be borrowed from the writings of theologian Paul Tillich (1886-1965), who referred to God as "the Ground of Being." By so designating deity, Tillich meant that, "God is not a being alongside others or above others but God is Being-itself or the Ground of Being."[27] Likewise, to Tillich, "God is not a being, not even the highest of all beings; he is being itself, or the ground of being, the internal power or force that causes everything to exist."[28] This conception of God compliments the way in which the New Spirituality conceives deity.

Even though Tillich's assertions about deity were esoteric and complex, Young presents a Tillich-like scheme of deity who describes herself as "the ground of all being" that dwells "in, around, and through all things . . ." (*The Shack*, 112) This view of God is acknowledged to be panentheistic (i.e., God dwells "through all things").[29] This may explain why, toward the end of his life, Tillich no longer prayed. He only meditated. To him there existed no personal or transcendental God to pray to. To Tillich God was immanent only—his "ground of being." So like an airplane, which is refused take-off for reason of mechanical failure, *The Shack's* concept of god never "gets off the ground." But, there may be a more startling similarity to *The Shack's* picturing of God.

Role Reversal

The feminization of deity extends back to time immemorial. The Egyptian goddess *Isis*, in which Matthew Fox finds precedence for the return of the *Black Madonna*, was the likely source for all the female god-images of ancient Middle Eastern religion, including the idolatrous "queen of heaven" worshiped by the women and men of ancient Israel (Jeremiah 7:18-20; 44:15-19). Interestingly, Young's idolatrous *Papa* goddess (a.k.a., "Elousia") finds herself in league with idol goddesses that Yahweh could not, and did not, tolerate before His face (Exodus 20:3-4). We now consider the second person of Young's trinity.

The Second Person

The Shack describes *Jesus* to be a quite human, a relatively unattractive Middle Eastern Jewish man with a "big nose" who functioned as the retreat center's repairman. (*The Shack*, 111) As regards Young's portrayal of *Jesus'* humanity, there is little disagreement. The author's portrayal of *Jesus* in a literary symbolic sense seems to fit within the bounds of Scripture (See Matthew 1:1-17; Romans 1:3; Isaiah 53:2; Mark 6:3).

Nevertheless, the author leaves the door open for the idea that *Jesus* originated from "Papa-mama." In explaining the derivation of woman from man, *Jesus* tells Mack:

> We created a circle of relationship, like our own, but for humans. She out *of* him, and now all males, including me, birthed through her (i.e., Eve), and all originating, or birthed, from God." (*The Shack*, 148)

Seemingly, this dialog makes Jesus' birth to be as common as the rest of humanity, thus calling into question His being the virgin born and "only begotten of the Father" (meaning unique, or only one of His kind, John 1:14; See Matthew 1:23.). Theologically, doubt is also aspersed upon Jesus Christ's eternal generation.[30] After this assertion, the novel pictures Jesus' desire to join all humans in "their transformation into sons and daughters of my Papa, into my brothers and sisters, into my Beloved." (*The Shack*, 182)[31] In this regard, never once in the novel is *Jesus* (His human name) ever referred to as "Christ" (His self-chosen messianic and divine name, Matthew 16:16).

Young presents his readers with a very human *Jesus* who comes up short of being Christ. We turn now to the third member of *The Shack's* trinity.

The Third Person

Sarayu, the retreat center's gardener—perhaps referring to Spirit's production of fruit for Christian living (Galatians 5:22-23)—is the character meant to represent the Holy Spirit. Just after his introduction to her, Mack asks *Jesus*, "Speaking of Sarayu, is she the Holy Spirit?" *Jesus* answers, "Yes, She is Creativity; she is Action; she is Breathing of Life; she is much more. She is my Spirit." Mack responds, "And her name Sarayu?" *Jesus* explains,

"That is a simple name from one of our human languages. It means 'Wind,' a common wind actually. She loves that name."(*The Shack*, 110)

Sarayu appears to be a Sanskrit word (the ancient religious and literary language of India). This language was, "Believed to have magical effects when spoken or even thought."[32] By naming the Spirit with the Indic word for "wind," the author appears to be alluding to eastern religion. The name may also allude to Jesus' comparison of being born to the blowing of wind which represents the work of the Spirit (John 3:8). But in naming the Spirit *Sarayu*, the author seems to allude to the *Rig Veda*, the Hindu scriptures, for semantically and phonetically *Sarayu* resembles *Vayu*.[33]

Nevertheless, the novel's impersonation of the Holy Spirit to be feminine contradicts Jesus' clear statement that the Spirit is neither an "it" nor a "she," but "He" (John 16:13-14).[34]

Yet, is there a fourth member of Young's trinity?

Wisdom

Though separate from the trinity, but secluded not far away from the resplendent retreat center, *Sophia* is a divine-like-lady judge who is the extension of "Papa-Elousia" and is all-wise in the ways god conducts his/her affairs (See Proverbs 8:1-36; 1 Corinthians 1:24.). In her verbal exchanges with Mack, she clearly possesses clairvoyant, if not omniscient, perceptions. (*The Shack*, 156, 160) Is *Sophia* a fourth member of the polymorphous godhead? Maybe . . . leave it to a reader's imagination.

CONCLUSION

Under the cover of biblical allusion, *The Shack* presents a god which may be compared to mythological deities. Readers ought to beware lest, by authorial slight of hand, they embrace spiritual delusion for reason of *The Shack's* biblical allusion. But you ask, "How could that happen?"

I would point out that Satan tempted Jesus via biblical allusion. In the second phase of the temptation of Christ, Satan referred to Psalm 91:11-12, to which Jesus responded by quoting Deuteronomy 6:16, "It is written again, Thou shalt not tempt the Lord thy God" (See Matthew 4:5-6, KJV.). Presenting a potpourri of spiritualities that combine biblical allusion with mystical delusion, *The Shack* will surely resonate with an Emergent Christian mindset that possesses no scruples about flirting with the New Age/New Spirituality. The fact that the novel is fiction makes no difference—it projects verbal imaginings that induce idolatrous images of God. As A.W. Tozer wrote:

> Wrong ideas about God are not only the fountain from which the polluted waters of idolatry flow; they are themselves idolatrous. The idolater simply imagines things about God and acts as if they were true.
>
> Perverted notions about God soon rot the religion in which they appear. The long career of Israel demonstrates this clearly enough, and the history of the Church confirms it. So necessary to the Church is a lofty concept of God that when that concept in any measure declines, the Church with her worship and her moral standards decline along with it. The first step down for any church is taken when it surrenders its high opinion of God.
>
> Before the Church goes into eclipse anywhere there must first be a corrupting of her simple basic theology. She simply gets a wrong answer to the question, 'What is God like?' and goes on from there. Though she may continue to cling to a sound nominal creed, her practical working creed has become false. The masses of her adherents come to believe that God is different from what He actually is, and that is heresy of the most insidious and deadly kind.[35]

To the Thessalonians Paul remarked how they, "turned to God from idols to serve a living and true God." Given the popularity of *The Shack*, we may be witnessing the evangelical church's turning from the "true and living God" to serve idols.

ENDNOTES

[1] William P. Young, *The Shack* (Los Angeles: Windblown media, 2007).

[2] Scripture also records that both Jesus and the Holy Spirit are also Truth (John 14:6; 1 John 5:7, 20).

[3] A.W. Tozer, *The Knowledge of the Holy, The Attributes of God: Their Meaning in the Christian Life* (New York: Harper & Row Publishers, 1961) 12.

[4] Peter C. Craigie, *The Problem of War in the Old Testament* (Grand Rapids: William B. Eerdmans Publishing Company, 1978) 95.

[5] Rev. Dr. Matthew Fox, "The Return of the Black Madonna: A Sign of Our Times or How the Black Madonna Is Shaking Us Up for the Twenty-First Century," *Friends of Creation Spirituality,* January 2006 (http://www.matthewfox.org/sys-tmpl/theblackmadonna/).

[6] Ibid. Article Number 1.

[7] Ibid. Article Number 8.

[8] Ibid.

[9] Ibid.

[10] Ibid. Article Number 6.

[11] Ibid. Article Number 7.

[12] The Wahine 'o Wānana Institute, "Hawaiian Goddesses, Goddess Papa," *Powers That Be,* (http://www.powersthatbe.com/goddess/papa.html).

[13] Ibid.

[14] In making this comparison, it can be noted that, having spent part of his life in what is now Indonesia, the author may have been familiar, whether consciously or unconsciously, with the area's indigenous spiritualities.

[15] See "Matt Interviews author of 'The Shack'," Wednesday, July 09, 2008, (http://carmpodcasting.blogspot.com/2008_07_01_archive.html).

[16] See Bridget Mary Meehan, *Delighting in the Feminine Divine* (Lanham, Maryland: Rowman & Littlefield Publishers, Inc., 1994) 20.

[17] "The designation 'Shaddai,' which some think is the oldest of the divine names in the Bible, occurs forty-eight times, thirty-one of which are in Job. The traditional rendering 'God Almighty' is debated. A consensus of sorts holds that 'shaddai' is to be traced, not to the Hebrew, but to an Accadian word that means 'mountain' so that the expression produces a meaning like, '*El* the One of the mountains.' If so, *El Shaddai* highlights God's invincible power." See Elmer A. Martens, "God, Names of," *Baker Theological Dictionary of the Bible,* Walter A. Elwell, Editor (Grand Rapids: Baker Books, 1996) 298.

[18] "El Shaddai as the breasted God," *SansBlogue* (http://www.bigbible.org/blog/2007/04/el-shaddai-as-breasted-god_12.htm).

[19] Emphasis mine, Meehan, *Feminine Divine,* 20.

[20] Ibid.

[21] Carl Schultz, "1560 עגל," *Theological Wordbook of the Old Testament,* Volume 2, R. Laird Harris, Editor (Chicago: Moody Press, 1980) 644. Schultz thinks that the calf might "have been a symbol of God's presence" among the Israelites. In this regard, I must compare the number of confessed evangelicals who, not content to walk by faith, are bent upon inducing a divine presence order to "feel" God. Can such discontent become a spawning bed for idolatry of goddess worship?

Seemingly, for the Israelites it did. After all, sexual feelings are some of the strongest possessed by humanity. The New Testament describes the pagan world as characteristically driven by the sensate, by lusts and desires (Romans 13:14; 1 John 2:16; 1 Peter 1:14; Jude 18). There is great danger when feelings, not faith, drive God's people.

[22] Ibid. Schultz also notes that the name for God (plural, *elohim*) might have been employed by the Israelites "in a pagan polytheistic way."

[23] U. Cassuto, *A Commentary on the Book of Exodus*, Israel Abrahams, Translator (Jerusalem: The Magnes Press, The Hebrew University, 1967) 420.

[24] Brevard S. Childs, *The Book of Exodus* (Philadelphia; The Westminster Press, 1974) 566.

[25] The Front Matter of *The Shack* posts rave theological kudos. Therefore, it is not unfair to evaluate the book's theology, especially the doctrine of God known to systematic theologians as Theology Proper.

[26] On this point, I find it interesting that the novel has not yet been accused of racial stereotyping, i.e., that God is pictured as being a "large" or "big black woman" (*The Shack*, 84, 86), and that Jesus comes from a Jewish nation of people with "big noses." (*The Shack*, 111)

[27] John P. Newport, *Paul Tillich* (Peabody, Massachusetts: Hendrickson Publishers, 1984) 108. Newport also observes that in the "grounding" of God, Tillich "seems to synthesize the pantheistic element of immanence with the theistic element of transcendence in a way that leans toward pantheism." (110) Newport's assessment may be too generous. At the end of his life, Tillich might have been an out and out pantheist. Of Tillich's book, *Courage to Be*, Erickson remarks that it "appears to have more in common with Hinduism than it does with historic Christianity." See Millard J. Erickson, *Christian Theology* (Grand Rapids: Baker Books, 1998) 334.

[28] Erickson, *Theology*, 333.

[29] For sake of explanation, pantheism teaches that God is all things while panentheism holds that God dwells in all things. For sake of analogy, a tree is not God (pantheism), but the sap which is the "life force" in the tree is. God is "in" the tree, but the tree is not God. See Erickson, *Theology*, 333.

[30] When it acknowledged Jesus to have been "begotten before all ages of the Father according to the Godhead," it might be construed that the Creed of Chalcedon (AD 451) allows for a concept that God originated Jesus (See http:// www. carm.org/creeds/chalcedonian.htm). However, to imagine the mystery surrounding the Trinity to be analogous to some kind of human begetting (i.e., as in the Mormon doctrine of Jesus' propagation) is improper. The relationship of the Father and Son to each other is their personal relationship, and it would be well for us

creatures not to invade their privacy (i.e., mystery). Their relationship is theirs alone. Though the unity Jesus prayed for among true believers may be compared to that of His with the Father, it is only similar to ("as"), but not the same as, their unity (John 17:21).

[31] In this regard, one can note the capitalization of "Beloved." When used in the NASB translation of the Bible, "Beloved" is capitalized as when Paul wrote of the grace God bestowed upon the believer "in the Beloved" (in Christ, Ephesians 1:6, NASB, NKJV, NRSV, 1901 ASV). Thus when the "Jesus" of *The Shack* said he desires people to be transformed "into sons and daughters of my Papa, into my brothers and sisters, into my Beloved" (*The Shack*, 182), it is as if Jesus envisions that humans can achieve a theotic state of "being" in which humanity merges into divinity. But the Bible teaches that while believers are "partakers of the divine nature" (2 Peter 1:4), they are not consumed of it (Romans 7:14ff.).

[32] Pat Means, *The Mystical Maze* (Campus Crusade for Christ, 1976) 203.

[33] "Word Mythology Dictionary: Vayu," *Answers.com* (http:// www. answers.com/topic/vayu-2).

[34] Those who desire to impute femininity to the Holy Spirit can only do so by assigning femaleness to the genderless noun, Spirit (Greek *pneuma*, neuter). But in doing so, they ignore the fact that Jesus referred to the Holy Spirit as masculine (John 16:13-14). The Lord said: "But when He (*ekeinos*, masculine gender), the Spirit of truth, comes, He will guide you into all the truth . . . He (*ekeinos*, masculine gender) shall glorify Me." So *The Shack's* feminization of the Spirit as *Sarayu* stands in direct contradiction to Jesus' referencing Him to be masculine.

[35] A.W. Tozer, *The Knowledge of the Holy*, 9.

FROM COSMOS, TO CHAOS, TO CONSCIOUSNESS
Quantum Physics and the New Spirituality

> Beware lest any man spoil you through philosophy
> and vain deceit, after the tradition of men, *after the*
> *rudiments of the world*, and not after Christ.
> (Emphasis Mine, Colossians 2:8, KJV)

The Shack

About the supposed "garden" which represents the state
of his life, Mack complains to the Holy Spirit, "Looks like a mess
to me."[1] (*The Shack*, 129) But from *Sarayu* (i.e., the "Spirit") we
learn that Mack's self-evaluation is only a matter of *his* perspective.
She informs him that his "messed up" life is really a fractal.

> "Mack! Thank you! What a wonderful compliment! . . .
> That *is* exactly what this is—a mess. But," she looked
> back at Mack and beamed, "it's still a fractal, too." (*The*
> *Shack*, 129)

The reader is left with the impression that God makes messes out
of the lives of Christians which can, depending upon one's
perspective, be fractal too.

But just what are fractals? *Sarayu* informs Mack:

> A fractal . . . is something considered simple and
> orderly that is actually composed of repeated patterns
> no matter how magnified. A fractal is almost infinitely
> complex. I love fractals, so I put them everywhere. (*The*
> *Shack*, 129)

Thus, *The Shack* incorporates aspects of quantum physics—chaos
(your garden is a *mess*), and fractal theory (your garden is a
pattern)—into its allegory. We will look at chaos and fractals, but
before doing so, we ought to note how the New Age Spirituality
has incorporated "chaos and fractals" into its worldview.

The Seeker

As evidenced in the movie *The Seeker*, quantum science has
given rise to quantum spirituality.[2] Based on the book *The Dark is*
Rising by Susan Cooper, the movie *The Seeker* portrays the story of a
adolescent boy, Will Stanton, the youngest of seven sons, who was
chosen by the wise and experienced "Old Ones" to seek for six

ancient signs that, if found, would enable the light to magically save the world from encroaching disaster and darkness, from chaos.[3] An ancient and mysterious book, which only Will the seeker possessed the ability to read, contained clues for discovering "the saving signs" that were hidden in past eras of world history. In one scene, which took place in the castle of light, Will read from the ancient book, after which both he and Merriman (one of the wise and experienced "Old Ones") commented.

> *Will Reading the Book*: "Six signs were created to contain the power of the light—from stone, bronze, iron, wood, and water. But the sixth was to be carried in the essence of a human soul? The signs were hidden and scattered throughout time. The seeker will find them."
>
> *Will Commenting*: "Okay. Look at this. <u>This pattern is a fractal. Its physics—my dad teaches this stuff. Like . . . like a hiding place that goes on and on forever.</u>"
>
> *Merriman Commenting*: "Like a clue hidden in plain sight that declares the presence of a sign." (Underlining Mine, *The Seeker*, Scene 11, The Book)

Will then asked for a hammer to shatter the object with the fractal design on it. After breaking it, he found a luminous stone on the inside—the first sign. Subsequently in the movie, fractal patterns indicated the presence of the other five signs that were vital to save the world from the chaos of darkness. Endowed with supernatural powers, and transcending time, matter, space, Will traveled into past eras of history to discover the other saving signs.

Because this book has been targeted for sale to a Christian market, some have accused *The Shack* of promoting New Age spirituality. On the face of it, when comparing the appearance of "fractal" in both *The Seeker* and *The Shack*, Paul Young does give the impression that, amidst the amalgam of other spiritualities woven into the fabric of his allegory, he is comfortable with the "science" of the New Spirituality. After all, the chapter in which the word "fractal" appears is titled, "A Long Time Ago, In a Garden Far, Far Away." (*The Shack*, 128) This provides the impression that, like Will in *The Seeker*, Mack in *The Shack* becomes something of a time traveler too!

To understand the relationship of the quantum aspects of chaos and fractal theory the New Spirituality, questions—like what is chaos and what are fractals?—need to be addressed. As derivatives of quantum physics, how are New Age religionists incorporating chaos and fractal theory to explain their vision of reality? Can this scientific-spiritual synthesis be squared to fit the biblical worldview? To deal with these questions, and to become aware of how some are deriving quantum spirituality from quantum science, a layman's knowledge of the quantum worldview and its disparate aspects of chaos and fractal theory will, I believe, prove helpful. After attending to these matters, we will biblically and theologically evaluate the way in which Aquarian spirituality is taking its quantum leap from *physics to metaphysics* and from *science to spirituality*. In order, we will look at the science, the spirituality, and the Scriptures. First, the science . . .

THE SCIENCE

The universe (Greek, *cosmos*) includes everything that exists, everything that's just "there," including human consciousness and understanding—though finite—of it all. The word "cosmetic" derives from "cosmos" which means "the world or universe regarded as an orderly, harmonious system."[4] We note the definition refers to everything—"the all"—as an *orderly system*. Just as with the rotating and tilting of the earth as it predictably revolves around the sun, "the system," on the face of it, appears to work orderly and methodically. But are things really that neat?

Well, it all depends . . . Who's observing, and how they are observing it? Physicists agree that *when looked at above*, from the macro-perspective, the system appears orderly and predictably (like a fractal). But *when looked at below*, from the micro-perspective, the universe appears to behave disorderly and unpredictably (chaos). We turn to the two views.

The Old Theory of Physics (a clock)

Derived primarily from the British mathematician and physicist Sir Isaac Newton (1642-1727), the older view looked at the big picture of things, at how large bodies of material and gravity interact. Newton observed there to be a predictable cause and effect relationship in the universe—that "everything happened according to fixed physical laws."[5] According to Newtonian science, reality was determined and ordered. Apples fall and, to use an earthbound expression, the sun dependably rose and set during a calendar year. By viewing the greater parts of the whole, the old physics appeared to confirm that God (the Clockmaker) originally designed, constructed, and wound-up the system (the clock).

When taken to an extreme, this view of reality leads to Deism, a belief that though a transcendent God created the universe, He abandoned it to let life work itself out on its own.[6] Built and energized in the past, the cosmos runs down in the present, and will, as determined by the laws of entropy, come to an abrupt halt sometime in the distant future. A universe that began will end. Newtonian physics viewed time to be *linear.*

The New Theory of Physics (a game)

But it is accused that the aging Newtonian worldview ignored contradictory evidence; that at the level of the smallest particles, the system behaves randomly. So a new quantum worldview has emerged postulating that the universe also behaves unpredictably and that time is cyclic, or *nonlinear.*

Stephen Hawking explains: "At the start of the 1970s . . . we were forced to turn our search for an understanding of the universe from our theory of the extraordinarily vast to our theory of the extraordinarily tiny."[7] At the subatomic reality of things, physicists calculated that quantities of matter and energy behave disorderly and unpredictably. Thus, the mathematics of quantum mechanics was born.[8] Whereas the symbol of the old physics was the picture of the atom consisting of protons, neutrons, and electrons neatly orbiting about, the images of the new physics are the complex mathematical equations and formulas by which physicists calculate the movement and properties of sub-atomic particles, or the manner in which quantities of matter and energy interact at the subatomic level.[9]

The Universe Described

How can the universe be explained? Do the math. The science of mathematics has been called the language of God. Centuries ago, Galileo Galilei (1564-1642), revolutionary Italian astronomer and physicist who discovered that the sun, not our earth, was the center of the solar system, stated, "Mathematics is the language with which God has written the universe."[10] Elsewhere, he wrote that to understand reality one needed to know the language of,

> this grand book—I mean the Universe—which stands continually open to our gaze, but it cannot be

understood unless one first learns to comprehend the language and interpret the characters in which it is written. It is written in the language of mathematics, and its characters are triangles, circles and other geometrical figures, without which it is humanly impossible to understand a single word of it [i.e., the universe].[11]

Dr. Francis Collins, longtime head of the Human Genome Project, in his book *The Language of God*, relates how, when he was a graduate student in chemistry at Yale, he took a course in "relativistic quantum mechanics" from Willis Lamb (1913-2008), who won the 1955 Nobel Prize in Physics. Spellbindingly and from memory, Dr. Lamb would move the students "through the theories of relativity and quantum mechanics from first principles." Intentionally and occasionally, he would leave out steps and challenge the students "to fill in the gaps" before the next class. Collins remarks that, "this experience of deriving simple and universal equations that describe the reality of the natural world left a profound impression on me, particularly because *the ultimate outcome had such aesthetic appeal.*"[12]

At what point in mathematics, it must be asked, does the aesthetic become mystic? Rothstein observes that, "In both mathematics and music, there have been notions of connection, linking the soul and the universe."[13] The German Johann Wolfgang von Goethe (1749-1832), once stated: "The mathematician is only complete insofar as he feels within himself the beauty of the true."[14] So in the monistic worldview of the New Spirituality, mathematics and music become sciences, aesthetic ways of knowing, by which people can develop a personal consciousness of feeling "oneness" with the universe, or with whatever else is just "there."

Among many mathematicians and physicists, hopeful optimism exists that an "eloquent and unified theory of everything" will be discovered.[15] Lucas remarks that's why "some physicists are busy trying to develop a Grand Universal Theory (GUT) which will unite quantum theory and the theory of relativity and become, as some put it, 'a theory of everything'."[16] The tool employed to discover a *theory of everything* is mathematics. If such an equation or formula be discovered, Hawking remarks:

> Then we shall all, philosophers, scientists, and just ordinary people, be able to take part in the discussion of the question of why it is that we and the universe exist. If we find the answer to that, it would be the ultimate triumph of human reason—for then we would know the mind of God.[17]

So at that juncture, mathematics jumps to become metaphysics. In fact, and though they may be running ahead of themselves, New Age spiritualists have already merged science and spirituality. The New Spirituality is taking the quantum leap from physics to metaphysics, from what is below to what is above.

When combined with data culled from other sciences—biology, chemistry, etc.—mathematics, with its signs and symbols, has become the newest and most sophisticated adventure to discover the intelligence of whatever or whoever might be considered God. But through the lens of Holy Scripture, how should we view this development? Consider with me the rightful place that nature plays in pointing any observer to God, and then some cautions about approaching God only on this basis.

We need to recognize that legitimate inferences can be made by human creatures about their Creator. For reason of our mutual but separate existences, Paul states: "since the creation of the world His invisible attributes, His eternal power and divine nature, have been clearly seen, being understood through what has been made" (Romans 1:20, NASB). The testimony is irrefutable, so much so that Paul states that *any* observer, from pre-historic to modern times, is "without excuse" (Romans 1:20b). In a limited way, physics relates to metaphysics. The physical evidence of the creation *below* points any contemplator of it to the Creator *above*. But we turn to consider some cautions and reservations regarding inferences about God that are derived from the study of nature.

First, God is infinitely intelligent. The Psalmist described, "Great is our Lord, and abundant in strength; His understanding is infinite" (Psalm 147:5, NASB; See Job 9:4; 12:13; 36:5.). As Paul first exclaimed and then asked:

> Oh, the depth of the riches both of the wisdom and knowledge of God! How unsearchable are His judgments and unfathomable His ways! For who has known the mind of the Lord, or who became His counselor? (Romans 11:33-34)

Are we to think that one day a physicist will develop an equation that will be an "eloquent and unified theory of everything"? Will physicist-mathematicians be able to fathom the unfathomable, to think equally God's thoughts, and become His counselors? I think not. Through Isaiah the Lord told Judah:

> For my thoughts *are* not your thoughts, neither *are* your ways my ways, saith the Lord. For *as* the heavens are higher than the earth, so are my ways higher than your ways, and my thoughts than your thoughts" (Isaiah 55:8-9).

A theory of everything? Believing in the Creator provides us with that! Why would anyone substitute a theory for God?

"I am the Alpha and Omega"

In the Apocalypse, the Lord God's name—"I am the Alpha and Omega"—expresses "not only eternity, but also infinitude, 'the boundless life which embraces all while it transcends all'."[18] (See Revelation 1:8; 22:13.) The title of "I am" designates that in His being, the Lord God transcends time. He is not subject to the chronology and sequential events of history. In fact, He controls them. Yet He is also immanently involved in time, matter, and space. He is "the Almighty." He is sovereign over the happenings of history. He holds "everything" in His grasp. One source remarks that the combination of the first and last letters of the Greek alphabet in ancient secular literature "came to designate the entire universe and all kinds of divine and demonic powers, so that . . . this title could refer to Christ's dominion over the universe."[19] So if physicists are looking for some Grand Universal Theory (GUT), then they need look no further than Christ. He says, "I am the Alpha and the Omega . . . who is and who was and who is to come, the Almighty'" (Revelation 1:8; See 22:13).

Second, Scripture informs us that visible nature bears an evident and adequate witness to God (Romans 1:20). Based upon the inferences and projections they calculate, and regardless what physicist-mathematicians might theorize or project about the design, order, or being of the universe, they too, like the rest of humanity, are accountable for what is plainly evident to them about God in nature. Yet some continue to pursue the science of mathematics not so much to bring God into the equation, but rather, to keep Him out![20] One scientist bluntly stated:

> Science, fundamentally, is a game. It is a game with one overriding and defining rule. Rule No. 1: Let us see how far and to what extent we can explain the behavior of the physical and material universe in terms of purely physical and material causes, without invoking the supernatural.[21]

Third, while the mathematics of physics can describe the design of the universe, it cannot account for the origin of it. Human knowledge is limited, even that of the most sophisticated observers who employ mathematics (i.e., the language of God) to explain the way in which they see the universe running. The scope of human knowledge is limited. The physics of the present cannot account for the metaphysics of the past. As God asked Job, "Where were you when I laid the foundation of the earth? Tell *Me*, if you have understanding, who set its measurements, since you know? Or who stretched the line on it?" (Job 38:4-5, NASB).

Fourth, knowledge (i.e., science) about God is for all people, not for two classes, the physicist kings and then "just ordinary people." Sophisticated scientists would do well to heed Paul's warning that, "not many wise according to the flesh" are called (1 Corinthians 1:26). All humanity, explains the Apostle Paul, possesses sufficient knowledge about God, "so that they are without excuse" (Romans 1:19). People tend to idolize intelligence, and if and when that happens, then human beings, cognitive beings that they are, will become self-worshipers, and as we shall see, this is already happening among the New Spiritualists.

Formulaic expressions of the quantum physicists can appear as esoteric and neo-Gnostic code language that only the scientific elite can understand. A friend of mine, a Ph.D. in chemistry, recently agreed that even within this special class of "knowers," there can be great ambiguity and disagreement about what's being communicated in the equations and formulas. One speculative physicist might not even understand the other.

While we recognize that many modern inventions and conveniences have come about for reason of quantum research—transistor radios, microwave ovens, and so forth—it needs to be asked: at what point do the calculations and theories become *futile speculation*? (Romans 1:21). To me, it's the point where physics begins to project into metaphysics. I know I will be scorned for saying this, but *physics does not unlock metaphysics*. While mathematics may support the intelligent design or teleological argument for God's existence, the mechanics of what is below, cannot account for who or what is above. To think otherwise is presumption, for the prophet Isaiah questioned, "Who has measured the waters in the hollow of His hand, and marked off the heavens by the span, and calculated the dust of the earth by the measure, and weighed the mountains in a balance, and the hills in a pair of scales?" (Isaiah 40:12, NASB). We will do well to heed the caution of John Calvin (1509-1564): "Therefore, let us willingly remain hedged in by those boundaries within which God has been pleased to confine our persons, and, as it were, enclose our minds, so as to prevent them from losing themselves by wandering unrestrained."[22]

Fifth, physics, while highlighting the design inherent to the structure of the universe, will in nowise reveal to us the personal Designer and Creator of the universe. That has been done for us in Jesus Christ, the incarnate and living Word, who by the power of His miracles revealed His mastery over nature's elements. Design points to Deism, and that's all. Intelligent design gives no verification of the Christian God who became incarnate by the Lord Jesus Christ. Thus, intelligent design can be equally employed to prove Allah as Jehovah.[23] And as some Christians might become enthralled by a fractal vision of everything, such an infatuation could corrupt them from "from the simplicity that is in Christ" (2 Corinthians 11:3).

God has spoken. "God, after He spoke long ago to the fathers in the prophets in many portions and in many ways, in these last days has spoken to us in *His* Son . . . through whom also He made the world (lit. 'ages')" (Hebrews 1:1-2). Though mathematics, anointed by scientists to be the language of God, may describe reality, it cannot account for the origin of it. No formula will provide to humanity a Grand Universal Theory. Only the Word accounts for the origin of "all things" (John 1:3), and this explanation of reality the Christian receives, not account of formulas conceived, but by the faith believed. Hebrews states, "By faith we understand that the worlds were prepared by the word of God, so that what is seen was not made out of things which are visible" (Hebrews 11:3). Only in the eternal *Logos* of God do we find the revelatory and reasonable account for the origin of everything. But into the perceived orderly working of the universe, some physicists have thrown a proverbial "monkey wrench."

The *"Uncertainty Principle"*

Whereas—viewing the universe according to largest scales of measurement (i.e., from the top down)—the old Newtonian physics saw "the system" as *ordered and determined*, quantum mechanics—looking at the universe from the perspective of the smallest scales of mathematical measurement (i.e., from the bottom up)—theorizes the system to be *unordered and undetermined*. By calculating mathematical formulas so complex that only elitist physicists can understand them, the new physics will only postulate probabilities, not absolutes. The cause-effect interaction of the smallest quantities of matter/energy (i.e., quarks, gluons, and electrons) appears to be uncertain and therefore chaotic.

Werner Heisenberg (1901-1976), a German physicist, theorized that, "we cannot localize a particle with arbitrary high precision and at the same know its exact momentum."[24] At the tiniest level of observation, accurate conclusions are impossible, for in the same instant of time—because both are constantly moving—a particle's position *and* velocity cannot be precisely measured. In the same millisecond either the position *or* the velocity of particles can be calculated, but not both. At the subatomic level, the flux of the one renders getting a fix on the other impossible. So just when you think you have it, you discover you don't. For example, maybe light is particle, or maybe it is waves. Depending on the experiment and who's observing it, light exhibits the properties of either particles or waves.

So a system, once thought to be determined, measurable, and predictable, now appears to be undetermined, immeasurable, and unpredictable. At the micro level, the random interaction of quantities of particles/energy introduces uncertainty as to how those parts might impact the "happenings" of the whole. When viewed from the bottom up, the only certainty about the universe is uncertainty. Science becomes a game, and life a bet!

So as physics morphs into philosophy, the uncertainty principle emerges as the template against which the entire spectrum of reality or life must be evaluated, including spirituality. As the Hungarian scientist-mystic Arthur Koestler (1905-1983) reportedly stated of the uncertainty worldview, "The nineteenth-century clockwork model of the universe is in shambles and, since matter itself has been dematerialized, materialism can no longer claim to be a scientific philosophy."[25] As New Age advocate Gary Zukav sees it:

> The world view of particle physics is that of a world without 'stuff,' where what is = what happens, and where an unending tumultuous dance of creation, annihilation, and transformation runs unabated within a framework of conservation laws and probability.[26]

A Quantum Question

According to physicist Stephen Hawking (1942-   ), reconciling certainty with uncertainty—as could be compared to the theological question regarding the relationship between determinism and human free will—is one of the great challenges facing modern scientific inquiry. "One of the major endeavors in physics today . . ." he writes, "is the search for a new theory that will incorporate them both—a quantum theory of gravity."[27]

In the chapter "A Piece of π," God asks Mack in *The Shack* about how freedom and determinism relate in life.

> Does freedom mean that you are allowed to do whatever you want to do? Or could we talk about all the limiting influences in your life that actually work against your freedom. Your genetic heritage, your specific DNA, your metabolic uniqueness, *the quantum stuff that is going on at a subatomic level where only I am the always-present observer.* (Italics Mine, *The Shack*, 95)

By her remarks it can be noted that "God" (i.e., *Papa-Elousia*) views her relationship to reality to be that of an observer, and not the Creator and Controller of the universe; and to be like that of a physicist, not the Sustainer of the universe. Nevertheless, the disparate chaos and fractal theories appear to be an attempt to reconcile irreconcilable aspects of quantum mechanics.[28]

Chaos Theory

A few decades ago, Edward Lorenz (1917-2008), discovered the mathematical aspect of chaos theory when,

> He inadvertently ran what seemed like the same calculations through a creaky computer twice and came up with vastly different answers. When he tried to figure out what happened, he noticed a slight decimal point change—less than 0.0001—wound up leading to

significant error. That error became a seminal scientific
paper, presented in 1972, about the butterfly effect.[29]

As Lorenz's discovery might seem to indicate, some
scientists now believe that the random interaction between
quantities of matter and energy in the micro-cosmos can affect the
behavior of matter and energy in the macro-cosmos. This
perturbation is known as "the butterfly effect." In the "dynamical
system" in which human beings are the conscious part, a butterfly
flapping its wings in the Congo could stimulate a wave/particle
disturbance causing a tropical storm in the Atlantic Ocean. Looked
at in another way, the first falling of a small domino somewhere in
the system could eventuate in the falling of greater and greater
dominos until the whole planet finds itself in state of chaos.[30]
Though in a closed system it appears that the smaller does
influence the greater, the magnitude of the impact of the smaller
upon the greater remains uncertain.

This is one hypothetical aspect of quantum physics known
as chaos theory, the theory assuming "that small, localized
perturbations in one part of a complex system can have widespread
consequences throughout the system."[31] But I call it hypothetical
because as the-physicist-turned-theologian John Polkinghorne
defines it, "Quantum chaology [is] . . . the not-fully-understood
subject of the quantum mechanics of chaotic systems."[32] In other
words, like the weather, one cannot assuredly predict the long
range effects of quantities of particles/energy interacting at the
sub-atomic level, and whether that interaction might affect the
greater part of the whole. A butterfly flapping its wings in the
Congo does not necessarily cause a hurricane in the Atlantic
Ocean.

Though the Newtonian view of the system (*order above
chaos*) is still viewed to be a player in the physics game,

> The world view of particle physics is a picture of *chaos
> beneath order*. At the fundamental level is a confusion of
> continual creation, annihilation and transformation.[33]

Linear Versus Non-linear Time
Quantum theory also influences one's view of time.
Previously understood as linear by the old view, *time is now viewed as
nonlinear*. As Emerging Church leader Leonard Sweet states: "We

do not live in linear time and space, but in curved time and space and nonlinear iterative processes."[34] Sweet then adds:

> Rather than stasis and order, the dynamics of life-systems are non-linear, where the rules of the game keep changing because the game keeps changing. One plays on the run and while everything is moving.[35]

Such a view of time explains why in *The Seeker,* Will became a time traveler, journeyed back in history, and found the fractal-marked signs by which the universe could be rescued from the encroaching chaos of darkness. This view of time may explain how Mack could visit a garden, "A Long Time Ago . . . Far, Far Away." (*The Shack,* Chapter 9, 128).

The Old Physics

The Newtonian worldview—that God the clockmaker made the universe to run like a clock—calculated time to be *linear.* One writer calls this view of time "straight arrow," and explains:

> Time marches in a straight line at a uniform pace from past to present to future, without variation. Time can only move in one direction—always forward, never backward, certainly not to the left or right, and never in circles.[36]

So tick tock . . . we're on the clock! According to the Newtonian understanding, the reality of life is sequential, chronological, and temporal. We were born. We live. We will die. This understanding accords with the Bible. The Psalmist wrote: "The days of our years *are* threescore years and ten; and if by reason of strength *they be* fourscore years, yet *is* their strength labour and sorrow; for it is soon cut off, and we fly away" (Psalm 90:10, KJV). Jesus spoke of "this age [and] . . . the *age* to come" (Matthew 12:32). At the time of His ascension, the disciples asked Jesus, "Lord, wilt thou at this time restore again the kingdom to Israel?" to which He answered them, "It is not for you to know the times or the seasons, which the Father hath put in his own power" (Acts 1:6-7). In light these biblical citations—more could be offered—it is concluded that the biblical "view of time may be called 'linear' . . . God's purpose moves to a consummation; things do not just go on or return to the point whence they began.[37]

Everything about life is sequential and therefore temporal. Time marches on . . . or, does it?

The Time Changers

Quantum physics introduces an alternative, though ancient, way of looking at time; that time is *non-linear*. This cyclic understanding of time opposes the biblical and Newtonian conceptualization of time.

Einstein's theory of relativity—that energy equals matter $(E = m)$—not only changed the understanding of the universe's material dimension, but also its temporal dimension. The quantum physical worldview theorizes that time is non-linear, or cyclic. Theologian Lucas explains:

> According to the theory of relativity time can no longer be regarded as an independent entity separate from the three spatial dimensions of length, depth, and height. Instead we have to think in terms of a unified, four-dimensional space time.[38]

Because outer space is measured by the distance that light travels in a solar year (i.e., light years), and because light may in fact be particles, quantum theory integrates light with space (because light is matter, and matter occupies space). Thus, a New Age spiritualist opines:

> According to relativity theory, space is not three-dimensional and time is not a separate entity. Both are intimately connected and form a four-dimensional continuum, 'space-time'.[39]

By combining time and space, and the energy-matter which occupies space, some scientists project there to have been no temporal "beginning" of the universe. There is no *ex nihilo* (out of nothing) origin of the universe. Everything just "Is." There is no God who, "In the beginning [time] . . . created the heavens [space] and the earth [matter]" (Genesis 1:1). The universe is just a gargantuan holistic and monistic "Oneness"—as above, so below. Stephen Hawking states:

> One could say: "The boundary condition of the universe is that it has no boundary." The universe would be completely self-contained and not affected by

> anything outside itself. It would neither be created nor
> destroyed. It would just BE.[40]

In this view of reality, time becomes cyclical and repeatable. This ancient religious and philosophical worldview, common to eastern religions, believes in an,

> endless return of golden ages alternating with dark ages.
> All that had happened yesterday and yesterday and
> yesterday would happen tomorrow and tomorrow and
> tomorrow.[41]

Rewinding their reality to the past (as in *The Seeker* and *The Shack*), or fast forwarding it to the future, become real possibilities for the human experience. Backward or forward, we can become conscious time travelers. We can control our reality providing we develop via prescribed mystical-meditative techniques, a new consciousness through which we can manipulate our reality from chaos to order (i.e., fractal). The science of the Mind can triumph over matter. As the cyclical complements the spiritual and the mystical, physics becomes the handmaid of metaphysics. Having looked at chaos theory, we turn now to the transformational aspect of chaotic mechanics—fractals.

Fractals

Polkinghorne notes that, "chaos theory is an odd mixture of order and disorder, of randomness contained within *a patterned structure*."[42] With his mathematically generated computer patterns, Benoît Mandelbrot (1924-   ) discovered what has become the other side of chaos theory.[43] The self-similar images reflect, it is believed, the self-forming capability inherent to the universe. These cloned, repetitive, and patterned images are called "fractals," the original Mandelbrot set being the most famous.[44] They are described as, "unique patterns left behind by the unpredictable movement—the chaos—of the world at work."[45] Though appearing chaotic (a mess), the system, from the minutest to the grandest levels, exhibits design (fractal-ness) everywhere—in cells, arteries-veins, nerves, body organs, snowflakes, mountain ranges, shorelines, ferns, roses, fruits, broccoli, leaves, and so on. Fractals allow the observer to sense the process of nature's *self-organizing character* and *inherent infinity*. Controlled by the numbers set into the equation, computer generated images can be observed replicating themselves *ad infinitum*.[46] The clones mimic infinity.[47] So it is theorized, from the chaos of the "Big Bang" [As terrorists know, explosions cause chaos], fractal emergence suggests that design, however random, can happen. The universe appears to possess an awesome power to replicate itself. Life is not doomed to end in chaos. There's hope! Out of the chaos (confusion), design (transformation) may haphazardly emerge. A source describes:

> Scientists have discovered that systems in transitional states between order and chaos possess certain patterns with unique, predictable qualities. These patterns are called "fractals." In essence, they are visual images or pictures of chaos at work.[48]

In their relationship to the whole, both chaos and fractals seem partnered in the cosmic process. As Sweet states:

> [We] live in a world that is ill-defined, out of control, and in constant flow and flux. We live in a world that is more weird than we ever imagined—a world that is fractal, self-replicating, inflationary, unpredictable, and filled with strange attractors.[49]

According to Jean Huston, a New Age advocate of human potential, "Fractals show a holistic hidden order behind things, a harmony in which everything affects everything else, and, above all, an endless variety of interwoven patterns."[50]

So according to this aspect of quantum theory, the world is not as hopeless as at times it might seem. As interrupted by chaos, fractals are observed to be coming and going. Chaos is a necessary prelude out of which fractal design will emerge. Our system is in a perpetual process of transformational change from disorder to order, disintegration to design, and confusion to creation. Fractals become the clues, the images, suggesting that life's reality is spirally evolving from a "mess" (chaos) into a "garden" (a fractal). Chaos is only believed to be a temporary phase of disorder that the self-transforming system, of which we are the conscious part, must pass through. Perhaps this explains why some evangelicals label their church emergent. The disorder that now seemingly besets Christendom only indicates the emerging of a new form of Christianity.

The whole process bears similarity to the Yin and the Yang of Chinese philosophy where, "the concept of yin yang . . . is used to describe how seemingly opposing forces are interdependent in the natural world, giving rise to each other in turn."[51] Amidst the chaos engulfing this planet, there resides the hope of fractal transformation. Hope happens.[52] So where physicists observe the system disintegrating and assuming fractals to be more science than art, they also see design (a "garden") emerging out of chaos (a "mess") everywhere. It's like looking into the patterns coming and going in a kaleidoscope.[53] As an aside, it might be noted that the geometric architectural constructions of Buckminster Fuller (1895-1983) also suggest his belief that design may emerge out of chaos.[54]

This brief description, from a layman's point of view, is an understanding of quantum physics and its attendant aspects of chaos and fractal theory. Yet quantum physics has also given rise to a philosophy of life, a worldview.

Dicey Design

As many know, Intelligent Design calls into question the Darwinian worldview and the academic establishment that espouses it. The anthropic principle, the idea that we live in a physical and biological universe so minutely calibrated as to enable human life to exist and survive, opposes the random philosophy of life implied by atheistic evolutionism.[55] After all, how can design exist without a Designer, the One the Bible introduces as God? (See Genesis 1:1.) Does our reality exist for reason of "chance," or the Creator? Are we to think that an explosion (chaos) in a printing shop produced the *Encyclopedia Britannica* (a fractal)?

The new physics with its attendant aspects of chaos and fractal theory, views such a lucky transformation as possible. Inherent within chaos is design. The planetary junkyard we live in may morph into a new car, provided the "green movement" can first prevent our earth from becoming a graveyard. The ecological crisis must be solved in order to buy the time necessary for the environment to evolve into a higher fractal form.

When the shift between Newtonian and quantum physics took place in the last century, Albert Einstein (1879-1955), believing in the old theory but fascinated by the possibilities of the new, protested stating, "God does not play dice with the universe."[56] Fractal-ism seems to be an attempt to account for the design in the universe absent a Designer . . . design by chance. Quantum-ism assumes that *a* self-originated, self-existent, and self-contained *system*, or universe, is also *a* self-creating, self-transforming, and self-evolving *complexity* continuously organizing from chaos into fractals. Reality is a continuum of disorder to order, order to disorder, disorder to order, and so on and so on, from infinity to infinity. The system, it is believed, possesses an inherent ability to transform itself. Order can emerge out of disorder, fractals out of chaos.

Dynamic Monism

So if hope exists, it resides in the ability of the system, in which human beings are the conscious part, to self-transform. Because of the way the universe works independent of the transcendent God, the worldview might be called, "dynamic monism." Though God remains materialized and energized in the cosmic processes—a sort of divinity does remain in, around, and through all things—He is depersonalized. No longer considered holy, God comes to be known by dynamic monists as "the Force," or the "It" of everything. This panentheistic and/or pantheistic view of life deny the sovereignty and providence of the Creator.

We can note the similarity of "dynamic-monism" to an ancient philosophy propounded by Anaximander (c. 610 BC–c. 546 BC). In his *City of God*, Augustine (354-430) noted the philosopher believed that,

> each thing springs from its own proper principle. These principles of things he [Anaximander] believed to be infinite in number, and . . . that [the principles] generated innumerable worlds . . . He thought . . . these worlds are subject to a perpetual process of alternate dissolution [chaos?] and regeneration [fractals?], each one continuing for a longer or shorter period of time, according to the nature of the case . . .[57]

In difference to intelligent design, Augustine noted that Anaximander did not "attribute anything to a divine mind in the production of all this activity of things."[58]

In the quantum view of reality, design just seems to happen, but some hypothesize that via human consciousness (presumed to be the cosmos' intelligent-control mechanism), humans can cause it to happen.

The Consciousness Connection

According to the old physics, humans were *observers* of the universe. According to the new way of understanding the universe, humans are *participants*. The New Spirituality hypothesizes that consciousness and cosmos are connected within a holistic universe, that spirituality and science, metaphysics and physics are interdependent aspects of the monistic and dynamic One. Not only can humans watch the universe operate, they also possess the ability to affect the happening of it. The German physicist Werner Heisenberg (1901-1976) for example, was one of the first advocates of the uncertainty principle. He is quoted to have said:

> The great scientific contribution in theoretical physics that has come from Japan since the last war may be an indication of *a certain relationship between philosophical ideas in the tradition of the Far East and the philosophical substance of quantum theory.*[59]

After all, if perchance God be removed from the system, what, or who, is left? Only the System is left, and the New Spirituality therefore calls upon humans, as the conscious parts of the System, to exercise their consciousness and play God.

THE SPIRITUALITY

To the new spiritualists, the universe is just "there." Within a universe seen as self-contained and self-creating, it becomes "natural" for an environmentally conscious New Age/Aquarian spirituality to combine philosophy with physics, to link *the cosmos* with human *consciousness*, to take the "quantum leap" from *the physical* to *the metaphysical*, and to combine *science* with *spirituality*.[60] Some even label the connection between consciousness and cosmos, *Quantum Spirituality*.[61] In his book *Soul Tsunami*, Leonard Sweet states:

> One of the greatest changes in perspective is the postmodern redefinition of size at both the gargantuan and the miniscule levels. *Physics is increasingly becoming the study of matter so small (is it a wave? is it a particle?) as to become the study of consciousness. In other words, physics is becoming metaphysics.*[62]

Generally, the existential leap involves three phases.[63]

First, any God—who is before, separate from, and therefore above the universe—is denied. Referring to the Jewish *Shema* which says, "Hear, O Israel! The Lord is our God, the Lord is one!" (Deuteronomy 6:4), a Rabbi explains:

> My genuine experience of life is that there is nothing
> 'out there.' This is all there is. And when you see the
> seamlessness of it all [monism?], that's what I mean by
> 'God.' . . . If you ask me what 9/11 really did, it made
> me understand the truth that, 'Everything is one.' Not
> that there's some guy hanging out there who has it all
> together, who we call 'One,' but that it is all one.[64]

In contrast, the Bible pictures reality as dualistic. God existed
before and separate from the universe which He created out of
nothing (*creatio ex nihilo*). Therefore, "below and above" is not a
"seamless whole." The God in heaven above is separate from earth
below. "In the beginning God created the heavens and the earth"
(Genesis 1:1). Jesus told those authorities who were His
antagonists, "You are from below, I am from above; you are of this
world, I am not of this world" (John 8:23). To believe it to be
otherwise, that "Everything is the One," is pantheism; and
pantheism is atheism.

God "In" Process

Panentheism (i.e., nature houses the divine Soul) is basic to
The Shack's view of God's being. For reality to be a "mess-below-
but-fractal-above," demands belief that a divine Soul infuses the
material universe; that the Soul is not only "around" everything,
but is also "through" and "in" everything.[65] Thus, Jesus explains to
Mack about "Papa-Elousia" in *The Shack*:

> *Being* always transcends appearance—that which only
> seems to be. . . . That is why Elousia is such a
> wonderful name. God who is the ground of all being,
> dwells in, around, and through all things—ultimately
> emerging as the real—and any appearances that mask
> that reality will fall away (*The Shack*, 112).

So "the ground of all being" who is a Papa goddess, "dwells in,
around, and through all things." Though it disavows that nature *is*
God (i.e., pantheism), panentheism believes that nature is
permeated with a divine Soul. For example, if someone hugs a tree,
they are not physically hugging God per se, but they are putting
their arms around an object that, along with the rest of nature,
houses the divine Soul. Thus, everything and everyone is endowed
with an aura of sacredness. Such a worldview, so the thinking goes,

will provide humanity with the spiritual basis and incentive to love one another, the creation, and thereby solve the ecological crisis.

Second, because they view reality as a monistic-seamless whole independent of "some-One-out-there," the New Spirituality deduces the universe to be a self-originated, self-contained, self-perpetuating, self-creating and self-evolving system "which is just there."

Third, how then, according to this systemic view of everything, are we to understand spirituality? Spirituality comes to be defined as an experience of feeling connected to and aligned with the Universe (i.e., the System, Nature, or Creation), the Source of everything that just *is*—as above, so below, as without, so within. One Aquarian spiritualist explains:

> Knowing that there's this interconnectedness of the universe that we are all interconnected and we are connected to the universe at its fundamental level . . . I think is as good a definition of spirituality as there is.[66]

To cultivate the consciousness of becoming and being *one with the One*, to feel connected to and aligned with the seamless whole of Nature, mystical experiences are necessary. Such spiritual encounters become means to that end. Something must happen to shift a person's inner consciousness to that of feeling connected to Creation, to awaken the dormant divinity that assumedly lies within every person. Mystical experience must transform sub-consciousness (below) into consciousness (above). So as one professor of religion explains, "Mysticism constitutes a core tradition within all the world's religions and is, above all, a positive and awesome *experience* of the mystery and miracle of being rather than hypothesis, inference, or mere belief about it."[67] Another states:

> In certain forms of mysticism, there is an experience of identification with every life form . . . Within the deep ecological movement, poetical and philosophical expressions of such experiences are not uncommon.[68]

Thus, we observe that the New Spirituality includes pursuit of mystical experiences through which contemplators—via techniques that include meditation, chanting, drumming, dancing, and taking drugs—can develop a consciousness of feeling "at-one-ment" with "the One" which *is* Nature, which is whatever is "there."

Likewise, while denigrating a biblical worldview as one of unnecessary institutions, arbitrary authority, and inhibiting rules, *The Shack* is big on experiencing "Creation" with a capital "C"—strolling in the garden, hiking in the forests, lying on a dock and looking up at the stars in the night skies, exploring caves, walking on water, and so on.[69] Thus a reader of *The Shack* is introduced to the role played by consciousness in the worldview of the New Spirituality.

Quantum Consciousness

Neale Donald Walsch peddles New Age spirituality in books recording dialogs or "conversations" he had with "God." The books are formatted so that his conversations and musings are typeset in normal characters while God's statements appear in **bold** print. Walsch notes one physicist,

> has proposed a conception of the universe that he has called "observer-participancy," or a closed-loop participatory universe in which—as quantum physics would have it—nothing that is observed is unaffected by the observer. In other words, the Creator and the Created are One, *each creating the other.*[70]

After stating that along with the rest of humanity, he is a conscious Part of the System, and that as one energy unit he can affect the System via intelligent-consciousness, Walsch states: "And then along come chaos theory and quantum physics." To this, Walsch's god responds:

> **Yes. And quantum physics is simply the scientific explanation for how God—"the System," if you please—looks at Its individual parts and watches Itself impacting those Parts.**
>
> **You would call this phenomenon, in spiritual terms, a "higher level of consciousness," or "increased self-awareness." It is when That Which Is Aware experiences the fact that It affects that of which It IS aware.**[71]

Walsch then muses, "'Nothing which is observed is unaffected by the observer.' The first law of quantum physics."[72]

According to the New Spirituality, if the system is to run right, the human mind is essential. Whether individual or collective, consciousness is the key. If the system should find itself in trouble, then human consciousness can become the means to transform, even save, the system. As has already been pointed out, the new consciousness can be induced by engaging in meditative spiritual exercises designed to empty one's mind and thereby create a mental state (i.e., a *tabula rasa*) in which fresh—perhaps environmentally sensitive—spiritual awareness can emerge. New Age spirituality believes that imagination and visualization, states of mind peculiar to the human species (the conscious part of the system), possess the power to transform reality. As stated in one New Age presentation on quantum spirituality:

> Your consciousness influences others around you. It influences material properties. It influences your future. You are co-creating your future.[73]

Again it is stated:

> I am much more than I think I am. I can be much more even than that. I can influence my environment, the people. I can influence space itself. I can influence the future. I am responsible for all these things. I and "the surround" are not separate. They're part of one. I'm connected to it all. I'm not alone.[74]

Consciousness affects cosmos; mind influences matter, perhaps to the extent that whether real or imagined, a person might take a quantum walk *on* water. (*The Shack*, 140-141) With the new awareness, expectation of help from outside the system, from God, becomes an "afterthought." Consciousness doesn't need the Creator because it is believed that consciousness is the creator (Contra 2 Peter 3:10-13.). Via the exercising of their consciousness (their inner divinity) and not unlike those within the Word of Faith Movement, humans suppose themselves to be gods.[75]

This mixing of science and spirituality results in a cosmic-humanist worldview which exalts humanity and diminishes the Deity. In fact, all that is needed to breed order out of chaos is that humans develop the resident control mechanism in their minds—the supra-consciousness, the Gnostic knowing—by which they as gods (i.e., "Christs") can stimulate the system to evolve to the next level (See Genesis 3:5.). In applying fractal theory to the potential of our species to evolve, one biologist states: "Evolution's repetitive, fractal patterns allow us to predict that humans will figure out how to expand their consciousness in order to climb another rung of the evolutionary ladder."[76] When achieved, this awareness is considered "enlightenment." Regarding the potential of a developed new consciousness, both individual and collective, it could be said, "They thought, and it was so." By developing their consciousness, humanity can create a brave new world.

This is how the New Age/New Spirituality attempts to cross fertilize with quantum physics. Like the discordant sounds of musicians tuning their instruments before a concert, the conductor (i.e., human consciousness) takes control, directs, and transforms the cacophony (chaos) into a symphony (a fractal). In a symphony of thought (a harmonic convergence), little "christs" can first imagine and then transform chaos into order. As Emergent Church leader Leonard Sweet puts it:

> The coming together of the new biology and the new physics is providing the basic metaphors for this new global civilization that esteems and encourages whole-brain experiences, full-life expectations, personalized expressions, and a globalized consciousness.[77]

In a recent article, Dr. Martin Erdmann concludes that since the late 1970s and early 1980s,

> spiritualization of science . . . has unquestionably made great strides. Its proposed change from a traditional value system based on analytical and rational thinking to a holistic view which imagines all aspects of intellectual pursuit to be in harmony with the mystical underpinnings of monism has led to the emergence of a global community having a heightened sense of cosmic spirituality that supposedly permeates all existence.[78]

THE SCRIPTURES
Contemplating the Cosmos

We turn now turn to evaluate, biblically and theologically, the new "scientific spirituality" and the worldview it promotes.

Because the universe is there—after all, we humans are the consciousness of it—questions arise. Why is it there? Why not nothing? The Bible gives a very direct answer to the questions: "In the beginning God created the heaven and the earth" (Genesis 1:1, KJV; Compare John 1:1 ff.).

The New Spiritualists presuppose that reality is "one thing" (i.e., monism), that it is "It." The historical Jesus however contradicted this understanding when He stated that reality consists of two worlds (i.e., dualism). To a divided and dualistic reality, Jesus gave the following witness to the Jews:[79]

> Where I am going, you cannot come? . . . You are from
> below, I am from above; you are of this world, I am
> not of this world. I said therefore to you, that you shall
> die in your sins . . . (John 8:22b-24a)

The things of earth lie within our ability to observe and understand. But heaven lies beyond our ability to observe and comprehend. While some things on earth below might be considered the shadow of things in heaven above, the one is not the replicate of the other (See Hebrews 8:5.). The reality of earth may infer the reality of heaven, but the realities are separate, not "one."

New Age spiritualists reject this understanding of the two realities. They suppose that reality is one unified sphere (as above, so below), that "here-is-there" and that "there-is-here." In their view, two different realities do not comprise the universe. The cosmos is but a divinized "One." Science and spirituality are viewed to be but two aspects of the same cosmic One. This humanistic holism ends up believing that whether in a pantheistic or panentheistic sense, nature is God.

Ain't So . . . As Above, So Below

But the Bible describes reality as two separate spheres; first, heaven above, the dwelling place of God, and then earth beneath, the abode of man. Only in the Lord Jesus Christ do the two spheres connect. New Ageism therefore rejects the belief in the one-time incarnation of the historical Jesus Christ who came from above (See John 1:14, 18). And this is, as John stated in his first letter, "the spirit of the Antichrist" which resides perpetually in this world. The apostle wrote:

> Every spirit that confesses that Jesus Christ has come
> in the flesh is of God, and every spirit that does not
> confess that Jesus Christ has come in the flesh is not of
> God. And this is the *spirit* of the Antichrist, which you

have heard was coming, and is now already in the world. (1 John 3:2-3, NKJV; See 2 John 7.)

Allow it to be stated that though God is "around" all things—He is omnipresent—He is not "in" or "through all things"—which is panentheism. If God is God, then the Creator-creation distinction must be maintained.

At the Temple's dedication, Solomon both asked and declared, "But will God indeed dwell on the earth? *Behold, heaven and the highest heaven cannot contain Thee*, how much less this house which I have built!" (Emphasis Mine, 1 Kings 8:27, KJV). Solomon's wise words put to flight any idea that matter is the panentheistic *container* of God.[80]

On Mars Hill, Paul addressed the Athenian philosophers and speculators, "The God who made the world and all things in it, since He is Lord of heaven and earth, does not dwell in temples made with hands; neither is He served by human hands, as though He needed anything, *since He Himself gives to all* life and breath and *all things*" (Emphasis Mine, Acts 17:24-25, NASB.).

The holy God is before, above, and beyond time, matter, and space, and is therefore transcendent and separate from His creation. As one theologian remarks of God's immensity:

> Just as in the case of eternity there was a qualitative difference between it and time, there is a qualitative difference between God's immensity and space. God's immensity is uncreated, and space [like matter] is created. Created space [and matter], therefore, cannot be the place of his residence.[81]

If it is believed that God indwells everything in the universe, then God's transcendence is sacrificed for immanence, and distinctions between the Creator, His creation, and His creatures are obliterated. If separation is ignored or denied, then the attribute of God's holiness—His being separate from His creation and creatures—is lost. Spirituality is left with sacred places, spaces, and times. But these are meaningless to the Holy God who as Spirit can be worshipped everywhere and all the time!

Neither does divinity reside in energy (i.e., the Force) and/or in matter (i.e., idols). This helps explain why Jesus mandated true believers to worship the non-locative and imageless

God in Spirit and in Truth (John 4:26). Idolatrously, both panentheism and pantheism materialize God in creation.

Quantum spirituality is based upon the world, not the Word, upon science and not the Scriptures. According to the New Spirituality, the opening of John's gospel might be paraphrased:

> In the beginning was the Cosmos, and the Cosmos was with Consciousness, and the Cosmos was Consciousness. The same was in the beginning with Consciousness. All things were made by It, and without It nothing came into being that comes into being. (My paraphrase, compare John 1:1-3.)

The Veneration of Creation

Deriving spirituality from quantum science obliterates distinction between the Creator and His creation. Upon the altar of idolatrous immanence, the transcendent and Holy God is sacrificed.[82] Instead of worshipping the Creator, quantum spiritualists venerate the creation (spelled nineteen times in *The Shack* with an upper case "C," 10, 94, 161, 222, etc.). In the first chapter of Romans, the Apostle Paul describes the substitution:

> For since the creation of the world His invisible attributes, His eternal power and divine nature, have been clearly seen, being understood through what has been made, so that they are without excuse. For even though they knew God, they did not honor Him as God, or give thanks; but they became futile in their speculations, and their foolish heart was darkened. Professing to be wise, they became fools, and exchanged the glory of the incorruptible God for an image in the form of corruptible man and of birds and four-footed animals and crawling creatures. (Romans 1:20-23, NASB)

The Colossian Heresy

Scripture warns believers against the veneration of the creation, against allowing a philosophy of human consciousness to intrude upon the worship of the Christ. To the Colossians Paul wrote:

> Beware lest any man spoil you through philosophy and vain deceit, after the tradition of men, *after the rudiments*

(Greek, *stoicheia*) *of the world*, and not after Christ. (Emphasis Mine, Colossians 2:8, KJV)

Though occurring in the New Testament only in this instance, the word "spoil" is a picturesque word meaning to carry off as booty or captives of war. As in the Babylonian invasion of Israel (586 B.C.), one can picture the captors, having plundered Jerusalem and seized its citizens, leading Jews bound in chains off to Babylon where they would be exiled and imprisoned for the remainder of their lives (See Jeremiah 31:15.). Likewise, Paul warns that if seduced by *the tradition of men* and *the rudiments of the world*, believers too can become spiritual captives. Just as the Babylonians took Judah captive by terror, so Paul warned that philosophy can take Christians captive by error. At the point of this warning, it ought to be noted that the word "rudiments" (Greek, *stoicheia*) possesses a physics-like meaning.

First, "the world" (i.e., the cosmos) is composed of "rudiments." As in modern physics, and as in the philosophical scheme of the ancients, cosmos or reality denotes "the sum total of everything here and now, *the (orderly) universe.*"[83] In part, the "*rudiments* of the world" comprise the essence of the universe.[84] O'Brien writes that in the phrase "rudiments of the world," *cosmos* is "understood to refer to the material, visible world while *stoicheia* denoted the elemental parts of that world."[85]

Second, outside the New Testament, "rudiments" is a physics-like term denoting "the four elements or the basic materials of the world [i.e., earth, fire, water, and air] of which the whole cosmos, and humanity within it, is composed."[86] To ancients, the word "rudiments" carried cosmological meaning. Thus, as opposed to "rudiments" (KJV), "elementary principles" (NASB); "basic principles" (NIV, NKJV), "evil powers" (NLT), or "elemental spirits" (NRSV), many scholars prefer the translation "elements of the world."[87] Employing such meaning, Peter predicted a time when the elements of cosmos would melt down. He wrote:

But the day of the Lord will come like a thief, in which the heavens will pass away with a roar and *the elements* (Greek, *stoicheia*) will be destroyed with intense heat, and the earth and its works will be burned up. Since all these things are to be destroyed in this way, what sort of people ought you to be in holy conduct and godliness, looking for and hastening the coming of the

> day of God, on account of which the heavens will be destroyed by burning, and *the elements* (Greek, *stoicheia*) will melt with intense heat! (Emphasis Mine, 2 Peter 3:10-12, NASB).

Third, from the context we note Paul warned the Colossians that fixating upon "the elements of the world" would lead them away from spiritual freedom and into spiritual bondage. In the quantum world, the ancient sense of "rudiments-elements" might be paraphrased to refer to something like "quarks," the smallest particles that some physicists believe are the quintessence of everything that comprises the material universe. However "rudiments" may to be understood—whether referring to particles, principles, or powers—the context demands an understanding that reverencing the physical essence of the universe can turn one away from worshipping Christ (i.e., "and not after Christ").

Thus, one scholar understands that "rudiments" can philosophically and spiritually refer to "the veneration of the *divinized elements* . . ."[88] If this be the case, then Paul is warning Christian believers not to allow something like a quantum physical worldview to corrupt their worship of Christ, Who is the One who created everything in the past, and Who is the One who controls everything in the present (Colossians 1:16-17). As to both its origin and endurance, the universe depends upon the Christ of God who "upholds all things by the word of His power" (Hebrews 1:3). So the apostle might be paraphrased to be warning, "Beware lest any man take you captive after the elementary particles of the world, and not after Christ." Christian spirituality should be based upon the Word, not upon the world; upon Christ, not quarks.

Cosmism and Christ

Yet as has already been pointed out, the new quantum spirituality does not seek to do this. It seeks rather, to derive its brand of spirituality from science, and its brand of metaphysics from physics. Consider the words of Matthew Fox who wrote:

> The Cosmic Christ is the "I am" in every creature. The divine mystery and miracle of existence is laid bare in the unique existence of each atom, each galaxy, each tree, bird, fish, dog, flower, star, rock, and human.[89]

In the view of Fox and other New Age spiritualists, the world should not expect a personal and physical Second Coming of the historical Jesus (Contra Acts 1:11.). Rather, they view that by cultivating mystical experiences, humanity will develop its collective consciousness that "a Christ spirit" or soul permeates the universe. To New Age spiritualists, Christ is Cosmos, and the developing of a collective consciousness that a divine Soul permeates the universe is, as the title of Fox's book implies, *The Coming of the Cosmic Christ*. By divinizing the elements, the new spirituality hopes that humanity will come to realize the sacredness of Creation, that nature possesses a quantum "I-am-ness" which, when understood by humanity, will save the planet from further exploitation and threatened extinction.[90] A developed consciousness of earth's sacredness, and not God, will save this earth from environmental catastrophe.

Captured!

Emergent Christians like Leonard Sweet, who allow their worldview to be influenced by such spirituality, are being taken captive by philosophy and vain deceit.[91] The "elements of the world" first enrapture and then capture their souls. Like Judah who played the harlot with other gods, their fixation upon science seduces them into spiritual bondage. Captivation with the cosmos leads to being captured by the cosmos, the very "system" which Scripture informs us, "lies in *the power of* the evil one" (1 John 5:19).

CONCLUSION

Investigation into chaos and fractals can turn a believer's mind and heart to the revelation of God's Word that describes His involvement in both the disorder and design of life. Any apparent mess in the universe does not occur independently from God, but rather happens in dependence upon Him. As Paul wrote, "For from Him and through Him and to Him are all things. To Him *be* the glory forever. Amen" (Romans 11:29). Though many have probed "the why" of God's relationship to good and evil (because the world contains evil, either God is not good—if He was, He would not have allowed evil—or God is not all-powerful—if He was, He would not have allowed evil), the Lord did say:

> I *am* the Lord, and *there is* none else, *there is* no God beside me . . . *there is* none beside me. I *am* the Lord, and *there is* none else. I form the light, and create darkness: I make peace, and create evil: I the Lord do all these *things*. (Isaiah 45:5-7, KJV)

Cosmos and Consciousness

Then there are the assuring words of the apostle: "And we knu that all things work together for good to them that love God, to them who are the called according to *his* purpose" (Romans 8:28, KJV). Amidst life which can seem chaotic at times, the sovereign God is working out His purpose in us. As one poet wrote:

The Divine Weaver

My Life is but a weaving
Between my Lord and me;
I cannot choose the colors
He works steadily.

Often He weaves sorrow
And I in foolish pride
Forget that He sees the upper,
And I the underside.

Not until the loom is silent
And shuttles cease to fly,
Shall God unroll the canvas
And explain the reason why,

The dark threads are as needful
In the Weaver's skillful hand
As the threads of gold and silver
In the pattern He has planned.

Author Unknown

As we confront the trials and struggles of life below, we are not privy to the pattern God is weaving above. We walk by faith (the just shall live by faith . . . without faith it is impossible to please God), and not by sight (Romans 1:17; Hebrews 11:6). At core, this is the error of quantum spirituality: what the observer thinks about the universe determines what the observer believes about the universe. What you see is what you get.

ENDNOTES

[1] William P. Young, *The Shack* (Los Angeles: Windblown Media, 2007).

[2] Because of her interest in cults, Jennifer Pekich rented the movie *The Seeker* to see if it presented New Age spirituality. Upon hearing the word "fractal" in the movie, and noticing fractal patterns marking the

presence of the signs, Jennifer remembered that she had seen the term before. After a brief lapse in memory, she remembered reading the word "fractal" in *The Shack*. At a conference in California, Jennifer informed Warren Smith of her discovery which he then communicated to me. Jennifer's awareness of and sensitivity to this connection, and Warren's communication of it to me, stimulated my inquiry into quantum physics, its aspects of chaos and fractal theory, and how the New Age/Aquarian religion was combining particle physics with spirituality. We are indebted to Jennifer for drawing our attention to the "fractal connection" between *The Seeker* and *The Shack*.

[3] *The Seeker—The Dark is Rising*, DVD, 20th Century Fox, 2008 (http://www.amazon.com/Seeker-Dark-Rising-Alexander-Ludwig/dp/B000XUUQRE). Reviewer Tami Horiuchi explains the plot: "Will learns that his destiny is as a seeker who must travel through time to collect six ancient signs [their presence marked by fractal patterns] that will somehow enable light to triumph over darkness and save the world as he knows it."

[4] *The Random House College Dictionary*, Laurence Urdang, Editor in Chief (New York: Random House, Inc., 1975 Revised) 303.

[5] "The Ultimate Paradigm Shift," *Fractal Chaos Crashes the Wall between Science and Religion* (http://www.fractalwisdom.com/Fractal Wisdom/index.html#paradigm).

[6] Unable to live with the theological tension created by the transcendence/immanence of God, theologians tend to swing from one extreme to the other, affirming either a creator God who is beyond nature (i.e., Deism) or a process God in nature (i.e., Panentheism). Both extremes deny Jesus' incarnation: deism by not allowing that Jesus, for reason of God's transcendence—His *being removed* from the world—could have come from above; and process-ism by demanding that Jesus, for reason of God's immanence—His *being involved* in the world—can only have originated from below. This is the spirit of "antichrist" (2 John 7).

Corduan describes the two theologies: "Like the God of deism, the process God does not intervene in the world. He is strictly finite. In the football game of reality, He is the cheerleader. He presents the world with ideals to aim for; He entices the world to follow His plans; He grieves if the world strays; but He cannot make the world do anything. As the world changes, He changes . . . Whatever He wants done needs to be accomplished by the world apart from His direct help." See Winfried Corduan, *Reasonable Faith, Basic Christian Apologetics* (Nashville: Broadman & Holman Publishers, 1993) 97. The process God bears close resemblance to "Papa-Elousia" in *The Shack*.

[7] Stephen W. Hawking, *A Brief History of Time* (New York: Bantam Books, 1996) 54.

[8] Comparing the universe to a municipality, Dr. Frank Stootman, in his excellent lecture "The Spirituality of Quantum Physics," defines quantum mechanics to be, "the mathematics of the very small end of town." His lecture is available at the *truthXchange* website (http:// www. truthxchange.com/sermon/the-spirituality-of-quantum-physics/). Another resource in understanding the relationship of particle physics to the new spirituality is, "QUANTUM MYSTERIES: Making Sense of the New Physics" (pp. 187-219), in the book *The Soul of Science, Christian Faith and Natural Philosophy*, written by Nancy R. Pearcey and Charles B. Thaxton (Wheaton: Crossway Books, 1994).

[9] See J. Trampetić and J. Wess, Editors, *Particle Physics in the New Millennium, Proceedings of the 8th Adriatic Meeting* (New York: Springer). The three-hundred and fifty-five pages of this book are filled with symbols and equations.

[10] Galileo Galilei, *QuoteDB* (http:// www. quotedb.com/quotes/ 3002). "'God is a Mathematician', so said Sir James Jeans . . . in the 1930s, the British astronomer and physicist suggested that the universe arises out of pure thought that is couched in the language of abstract mathematics." See F. David Peat, "Mathematics and the Language of Nature," *fdavidpeat.com* (http:// www. fdavidpeat.com/bibliography/essays/ maths.htm). His essay was originally published in *Mathematics and Sciences*, edited by Ronald E. Mickens (Word Scientific, 1990).

[11] Ibid. (http:// www. quotedb.com/quotes/510).

[12] Emphasis mine, Francis S. Collins, *The Language of God, A Scientist Presents Evidence for Belief* (New York: Free Press, 2006) 61-62. Explaining the mystery that surrounds matter's behavior, Collins asks, borrowing a phrase from Hungarian-American and mathematician-physicist Eugene Wigner (1902-1995), "what could be the explanation for the 'unreasonable effectiveness of mathematics'?"

[13] Edward Rothstein, *Emblems of Mind, The Inner Life of Music and Mathematics* (New York: Avon Books, 1995) 30.

[14] Ibid. quoting Von Goethe, 135.

[15] Collins, *Language of God*. Similarly, the father of modern mathematics, Pierre Simon, Marquis de Laplace (1749-1827) theorized that, "An intelligence which at a given instant knew all the forces acting in nature and the position of every object in the universe . . . could describe with a single formula the motions of the largest astronomical bodies and those of the smallest atoms. To such an intelligence, nothing would be uncertain; the future, like the past, would be an open book." See "Science Quotes by Pierre Simon, Marquis de Laplace," *Today in Science History* (http:// www. todayinsci.com/L/Laplace_Pierre/LaplacePierre-Quotations.htm).

¹⁶ Ernest C. Lucas, "God, GUTs and Gurus: the New Physics and New Age Ideology," *Themelios* 16:3 (April/May 1991) 7. Article is available online at (http:// s3.amazonaws.com/tgc-documents/journal-issues/16.3_Lucas.pdf). Likewise Carson observes, "that some physicists hope the discovery of the long-sought unifying equation will in principle explain everything in the universe mathematically . . ." See D.A. Carson, *The Gagging of God* (Grand Rapids: Zondervan Publishing House, 1996) 199.

¹⁷ Ibid. Collins quotes S. Hawking, *A Brief History of Time* (New York: Bantam Press, 1998) 210.

¹⁸ Robert L. Thomas, *Revelation: An Exegetical Commentary*, Volume I (Chicago: Moody Press, 1992) 81. Thomas here quotes H.B. Swete, *The Apocalypse of St. John* (London: Macmillan, 1906) 11.

¹⁹ Johannes P. Louw and Eugene A. Nida, *Greek-English Lexicon of the New Testament Based on Semantic Domains*, Volume I (New York: United Bible Societies, 1989) 61.7, *alpha*, 611.

²⁰ Ben Laake, "*Our Quantum Reality: The Mathematics of the Mechanics*" (http:// herescope.blogspot.com/2009/05/our-quantum-reality.html).

²¹ Carson, *Gagging of God*, 195, quoting Richard E. Dickerson, "The Game of Science," *Perspectives on Science and Faith* 44 (June 1992): 137.

²² John Calvin, *Institutes of the Christian Religion*, Translated by Henry Beveridge (Grand Rapids: Wm. B. Eerdmans Publishing Company, Reprinted 1972) I. xiv. 1.

²³ On this point I find myself at variance with Christian mathematician Jason Lisle who wrote: "A biblical creationist expects to find beauty and order in the universe, not only in the physical universe, but in the abstract realm of mathematics as well. This order and beauty is possible because there is a logical God who has imparted order and beauty into His universe." True. In the abstract symmetry of the physical universe, one may be led to believe in a logical God, but it is not consequent that, as exhibited by Christ, the believer will view God to be personal and spiritual. See Jason Lisle, Ph.D., "Fractals: Hidden Beauty Revealed in Mathematics," *answersingenesis.org*, January 1, 2007 (http:// www. answersingenesis.org/articles/am/v2/n1/fractals)

²⁴ Peter Schupp, "Particle Physics on Noncommutative Space-Time," *Physics in the New Millennium*, 305.

²⁵ Arthur Koestler, *Research in Parapsychology* 1972 (special dinner address), quoted by Dave Hunt, *A Cup of Trembling* (Eugene, Oregon: Harvest House Publishers, 1995) 373.

²⁶ Gary Zukav, *Dancing Wu Li Masters, An Overview of the New Physics* (New York: Harper Collins Publishers, Inc., 2001) 217.

[27] Stephen W. Hawking, *A Brief History of Time, From the Big Bang to Black Holes* (New York: Bantam Books, 1988) 12. de Laplace too surmised that, "Given for one instant an intelligence which could comprehend all the forces by which nature is animated and the respective positions of the beings which compose it, if moreover this intelligence were vast enough to submit these data to analysis, it would embrace in the same formula both the movements of the largest bodies in the universe [i.e., the old Newtonian physics] and those of the lightest atom [the new quantum physics]; to it nothing would be uncertain, and the future as the past would be present to its eyes [the concept of time becomes non-linear]. See "Science Quotes."

[28] See James Gleick, *Chaos, Making a New Science* (New York: Penguin Books, 1987). The terms chaos and fractal occur frequently in the book.

[29] See "MIT prof Edward Lorenz, father of chaos theory, dies at 90," *Muzi.com. News*, April 16, 2008 (http:// lateline.muzi.net/news/ll/ english/10066912.shtml?cc=11176).

[30] Theoretically, the detonation of a nuclear device could lead to spontaneous and uncontrolled combustion melting down the whole planet.

[31] John M. Last, "Chaos Theory," *enotes.com* (http:// www. enotes.com/public-health-encyclopedia/chaos-theory).

[32] John Polkinghorne, *Quantum Theory, A Very Short Introduction* (New York: Oxford University Press, 2002) 97.

[33] Zukav, *Wu Li Masters*, 216.

[34] Leonard Sweet, *SoulTsunami, Sink or Swim in New Millennium Culture* (Grand Rapids: Zondervan, 1999) 80.

[35] Ibid.

[36] J.M. Berger, "Flashbacks, Memory and Non-Linear Time," *Lost Online Studies* (http:// www. loststudies.com/1.2/memory-and-time.html).

[37] M.H. Cressey, "Time," *The New Bible Dictionary*, J.D. Douglas, Editor (Grand Rapids: Wm. B. Eerdmans Publishing Co., 1962) 1277.

[38] Lucas, "God, GUTs and Gurus."

[39] Fritjof Capra, *The Tao of Physics, An Exploration of the Parallels between Modern Physics and Eastern Mysticism*, 4th Edition Updated (Boston: Shambhala Publications, Inc., 1999) 62.

[40] Hawking, *A Brief History of Time*, 136

[41] Edward Harrison, *Masks of the Universe, Changing Ideas on the Nature of the Cosmos*, Second Edition (New York: Cambridge University Press, 2003) 104-105.

⁴² Emphasis Mine, John Polkinghorne, *Quarks, Chaos & Christianity, Questions to Science and Religion* (New York: The Crossroad Publishing Company, 1996) 67.

⁴³ "Benoît Mandelbrot," *Wikipedia* (http:// en. wikipedia.org/ wiki/Beno%C3%AEt_Mandelbrot). See too "Mandelbrot set" (http:// en. wikipedia.org/wiki/Mandelbrot_set).

⁴⁴ Generated by computers, variations of the Mandelbrot set may be observed at the website *Fractal Geometry*. (http:// mail. colonial.net/~ abeckwith/fractals.html). Computer generated fractals are truly beautiful works of art that tantalize both the eye and the soul.

⁴⁵ Borders Books' definition of "fractals" in the locater- monitor's description of John Briggs' book, *Fractals: The Patterns of Chaos* (New York: Touchstone, Simon & Schuster, Inc., 1992).

⁴⁶ As Lisle explains, "A fractal contains an infinite number of copies of itself . . . The Mandelbrot set is infinitely detailed . . . on the 'tail' of the Mandelbrot set . . . we find but another (smaller) version of the original. This new, smaller Mandelbrot set also has a tail containing a miniature version of itself, which has a miniature version of itself, etc.— all the way to infinity. The Mandelbrot set is called a 'fractal' since it has an infinite number of its own shape built into itself." See Jason Lisle, "Fractals." Fractals do not though, it seems to me, account for the variation within creation.

⁴⁷ Ibid. In his analysis of the Mandelbrot set and asserting there exists in numbers a "secret code," Lisle employs the words, "infinitely . . . infinity."

⁴⁸ Borders Books.

⁴⁹ Sweet, *SoulTsunami*, 80.

⁵⁰ Jean Houston, *A Mythic Life* (New York: Harper Collins Publishers, Inc., 1996) 7. As another defines them, "In the most basic sense, fractals are defined as small parts that represent the whole while displaying the same level of complexity at any scale. One other definition of fractals is that they are mathematical models that mimic nature." See Dr. Horace Campbell, "Think Piece, Barack Obama, Fractals, and Momentum in Politics," *The Black Commentator* (http:// www. black commentator.com/265/265_obama_fractals_momentum_campbell_thin k.html).

⁵¹ "Yin and yang," *Wikipedia*, http:// en. wikipedia.org/wiki/ Yin_yang.

⁵² In his book, *Everything Must Change, Jesus, Global Crises, and a Revolution of Hope* (Nashville: Thomas Nelson, 2007), Brian D. McLaren titles the first chapter "Hope Happens." He frequently employs the statement in the book.

[53] One can also observe kaleidoscopic and fractal-like designs in both Indian and African art. See (http:// upload.wikimedia.org/ wikipedia/en/8/8b/Buddhabrot-deep.jpg) and (https:// maigida.com/).

[54] The Unitarian R. Buckminster Fuller preoccupied himself with the question, "Does humanity have a chance to survive lastingly and successfully on planet Earth, and if so, how?" See Bill McKibben, Editor, *Environmental Earth, Environmental Writing Since Thoreau* (U.S.A.: Penguin Group, 2008) 464. Evidently, he found hope through his calculated geodesic and tetrahedral designs. In his 1968 book, *I Seem to Be a Verb*, he wrote: "I live on Earth at present, and I don't know what I am. I know that I am not a category. I am not a thing—a noun. I seem to be a verb, an evolutionary process –an integral function of the universe." In Fuller's worldview, human survival depends upon design emerging from chaos. It should be noted that William Young approvingly quotes Fuller. (*The Shack*, 194) Scripture does teach that God will create the new heavens and the new earth out of the chaos of a fallen creation (Isaiah 65:17; 2 Peter 3:11-13; Revelation 21:1; Romans 8:21).

[55] See William A. Dembski, *Intelligent Design, The Bridge Between Science & Theology* (Downers Grove, Illinois: InterVarsity Press, 1999). In this book's "Foreword," Michael J. Behe summarizes that physically, "the universe is fine-tuned for life, ranging from the strength of the gravitational constant to the values of the resonance levels of carbon nuclei to the frequency of supernovae." He also points out that biologically, design lies at "the cellular basis of life, where molecular machines of stunning complexity carry out life's most basic tasks." (p. 11).

[56] Thomas Torrance, "Reflections: Einstein and God," *Center of Theological Inquiry* (http:// 74.125.95.132/search?q=cache:dnWCKtO3 JPUJ:www. ctinquiry.org/publications/reflections_volume_1/torrance. htm+Einstein,+%22dice%22&hl=en&ct=clnk&cd=3&gl=us).

[57] Augustine, "City of God," *Great Books of the Western World*, Volume 18, Robert Maynard Hutchins, Editor in Chief (Chicago: Encyclopaedia Britannica, Inc,) Book VIII, Chapter 2, page 265.

[58] Ibid.

[59] Emphasis Mine, Werner Heisenberg quoted by Fritjof Capra, *The Tao of Physics*, 18. Capra also quotes Quantum physicists Julius Robert Oppenheimer and Niels Bohr with the supposition that quantum mechanics and quantum mysticism compliment one another. In other words, there is a quantum link between science and spirituality!

Philosopher Ken Wilbur on the other hand, thinks that merging particle physics to mystical spirituality is in error. Though many quantum physicists were mystics, they were not so for reason of science. Wilbur rejects the "physics-supports-mysticism" idea because of the "uncertainty" that quantum theory is science's final view of reality. Like quantum theory has done to the old Newtonian worldview, one day it too will probably be superseded by some new theory of reality, and if this should happen, then Wilbur knows that any spirituality connected to the quantum worldview would be trumped and rendered obsolete. See Ken Wilbur, Editor, *Quantum Questions, Mystical Writings of the World's Great Physicists* (Boston: Shambhala, 1985) ix.

[60] J.C. Polkinghorne notes that, "Two books which survey modern physics and seek to assimilate it to Eastern thought are Fritjof Capra: *The Tao of Physics* (Fontana, 1976), Gary Zukav: *The Dancing Wu Li Masters* (Fontana, 1980)." Polkinghorne then gives his estimation of the attempt. He writes: "Personally I feel that the attempt depends too greatly on purely verbal parallels to be convincing." *The Quantum World* (Princeton, New Jersey: Princeton University Press, 1984) 97.

[61] Leonard I. Sweet, *Quantum Spirituality, A Post Modern Apologetic* (Dayton, Ohio: Whaleprints, 1991).

[62] Emphasis Mine, Sweet, *SoulTsunami*, 109.

[63] Blackburn states notes that, "Existentialist writing . . . reacts against the view that the universe is a closed, coherent, intelligible system [i.e., that of the old Newtonian physics] . . . In the face of an indifferent universe we are thrown back upon our own freedom. Acting authentically becomes acting in the light of the open space of possibilities that the world allows." See Simon Blackburn, "existentialism, "*Oxford Dictionary of Philosophy* (New York: Oxford University Press, 2005) 125.

[64] Rabbi Irwin Kula quoted by William J. Jackson, *Heaven's Fractal Net, Retrieving Lost Visions in the Humanities* (Bloomington, Indiana: Indiana Press, 2004) 239-240.

[65] On this point Rick Warren quotes the *New Century Version's* theologically errant rendition of Ephesians 4:6b, that God "rules everything and is everywhere and *is in everything*" (Italics Mine). See *The Purpose Driven Life* (Grand Rapids: Zondervan, 2002) 88.

[66] Stuart Hameroff, M.D., *What the Bleep do we know!?* DVD (Beverly Hills, California: © 20th Century Fox, 2004).

[67] Paul Brockelman, *Cosmology and Creation, The Spiritual Significance of Contemporary Cosmology* (New York; Oxford University Press, 1999) 74.

[68] Ibid. 153. Quoting Arne Naess, "Identification as a Source of Deep Ecological Attitudes," in *Deep Ecology*, Michael Tobias, Editor (San Diego: Avant Books, 1985) 153.

[69] It can be counted that the word "creation" occurs approximately twenty times in *The Shack*, and is always spelled with a capital "C." By his use of the upper case spelling contra Romans 1:25, is the author assigning divinity to nature? In the first occurrence of the word "nature," it too is spelled with a capital "N." (*The Shack*, 15) On the preceding page, Young also wrote of "the god of winter." (*The Shack*, 14)

[70] Neale Donald Walsch, *Tomorrow's God, Our Greatest Spiritual Challenge* (New York: Atria Books, 2004) 24.

[71] Ibid. 84.

[72] Ibid. 85.

[73] *What the Bleep do we know!?* DVD (Beverly Hills, California: © 20th Century Fox, 2004).

[74] Ibid.

[75] Members of the Word of Faith Movement believe that through the power of their spoken word they as little gods they can "name it and claim it." The daughter of Charles Capps writes in her booklet, "Your words are energy and they affect the matter in your life." Again, "The thoughts and beliefs that you carry also produce energy around you." And again, "Faith is an unseen energy force. It is not matter, but it creates matter and actually becomes matter." See Annette Capps, *Quantum Faith* (England, Arkansas: Capps Publishing, 2003) 7, 9, 22.

[76] Bruce H. Lipton, *The Biology of Belief, Unleashing the Power of Consciousness, Matter & Miracles* (Carlsbad, California: Hay House, Inc., 2008) 168.

[77] Sweet, *SoulTsunami*, 121.

[78] Martin Erdmann, "The Spiritualization of Science, Technology, and Education in a One-World Society," *European Journal of Nanomedicine*. Volume 2, 2009, 36 (http://www.clinam.org/journal/index.php/NanoJournal/article/view/.7/33). See also (http://herescope.blogspot.com/2009/05/spiritualization-of-science.html).

[79] If the two separate realities of heaven and earth are merged into one thing that's there (i.e., monism), then not only is the Holy God compromised (paving the way for idolatry), but also the incarnation of God in Jesus is made impossible and unnecessary. After all, how can we speak of Jesus coming into the world if a so-called "cosmic Christ" like that envisioned by Matthew Fox was/is pervasively present in the world?

[80] The Hebrew word for "contain" (e.g., kûl) means "to contain as a vessel." See John N. Oswalt, "962 כול (kûl)," *Theological Wordbook of the Old Testament*, R. Laird Harris, Editor (Chicago: Moody Press, 1980) 1.432.

[81] Morton H. Smith, *Systematic Theology*, Volume One (Greenville, South Carolina: Greenville Seminary Press, 1994) 135.

[82] See Essay #2 in this booklet, "The Holy God, Immanence to Idolatry," pp. 17-22.

[83] Walter Bauer, *A Greek-English Lexicon of the New Testament and Other Early Christian Literature*, William F. Arndt and F. Wilbur Gingrich, Translators, Revised by F. Wilbur Gingrich and Frederick W. Danker (Chicago: The University of Chicago Press, 1979) 445.

[84] Daniel B. Wallace, *Greek Grammar Beyond the Basics* (Grand Rapids: Zondervan Publishing House, 1996) 84-86. In the phrase

"rudiments of the world," the genitive "world" (*tou kosmou*) seems to be the whole of which the "rudiments" (*ta stoicheia*) are parts.

[85] Peter T. O'Brien, *Word Biblical Commentary, Volume 44 Colossians, Philemon* (Waco, Texas: Word Books, 1982) 131.

[86] G. Delling, "stoicheion," *Theological Dictionary of the New Testament*, Gerhard Kittel and Gerhard Friedrich, Editors, Geoffrey W. Bromiley, Translator, Abridged in One Volume by Geoffrey W. Bromiley (Grand Rapids: William B. Eerdmans Publishing Company, 1985) 1088. Because of the word's common meaning in that day, Delling adds, "Only the context can yield any other sense."

[87] See Robert W. Wall, *Colossians & Philemon* (Downers Grove: InterVarsity Press, 1993) 107.

[88] Emphasis Mine, Clinton E. Arnold, *The Colossian Syncretism, The Interface between Christianity and Folk Belief at Colossae* (Grand Rapids: Baker Books, 1996) 189.

[89] Matthew Fox, *The Coming of the Cosmic Christ, The Healing of Mother Earth and the Birth of a Global Renaissance* (San Francisco: Harper Collins Publishers, 1980) 154.

[90] Ibid.

[91] Sweet cites and refers readers to the works of Matthew Fox in *Quantum Spirituality*. (324) On this point we should note that then Cardinal Joseph Ratzinger, now Pope Benedict XVI, forbade Fox to teach theology in 1988, after which he was dismissed from the Dominican order in 1992.

THE SHACK AND UNIVERSAL RECONCILIATION[1]
Rebels, Rules, and Reconciliation

> Now then we are ambassadors for Christ, as though God did beseech *you* by us: we pray *you* in Christ's stead, be ye reconciled to God. (2 Corinthians 5:20, KJV)

Reconciliation means a change in "relationship."[2] The need for reconciliation presupposes estrangement between two parties (Matthew 5:23-24). Whereas they became enemies, two parties become friends again. Often, reconciliation needs to occur between humans, between friends, spouses, races, tribes, and nations. But reconciliation also needs to take place between people and God. Though Paul stated that the Colossians were "reconciled," he noted that in their former state they had been spiritually "alienated" from God for reason of their rebellion against Him (Colossians 1:21-22). Because of sinfulness, people are universally separated from God and need to be reconciled with Him. As such, the doctrine of reconciliation is core to the Christian faith. As White remarks, "Since a right relationship with God is the heart of all religion, reconciliation, which makes access welcome and fellowship possible, may be regarded as the central concept in Christianity."[3]

In contrast to those who are "enemies of the cross of Christ" and "lovers of pleasure rather than lovers of God" (Philippians 3:18; 2 Timothy 3:4), the Bible calls faithful Abraham "the friend of God" (James 2:23; Romans 4:3). In their relationship to God, all humanity falls into two groups: they are either His friends or His enemies. Either they are reconciled to God, or they are not. *The Shack* therefore, is big on relationships.[4]

In a conversation between members of the trinity and Mack, *Sarayu* tells him (though *Papa* might be speaking), "Mackenzie, we have no concept of final authority among us, only unity. We are a *circle* of relationship . . ." (*The Shack*, 122) Dismissing any idea of hierarchy or subordination amongst members of the trinity, *Papa-Elousia* later explains to Mack that, "Submission . . . is all about relationships of love and respect." (*The Shack*, 145) The vaguely Christian underpinnings of the book, and its emphasis upon relationship on the one hand and its de-emphasis of rules on the other, requires that the connection between law and the Christian life be examined.

Rules and Relationships

In cavalier fashion, the novel dismisses the relevance of rules (i.e., law) to relationship (i.e., love). (*The Shack*, 7, 122, 123, 197-205) The "all-God-cares-about-is relationship" theory renders rules to be obsolete ("Kum Ba Ya"). *Sarayu* even states to Mack, "The Bible doesn't teach you to follow rules." (*The Shack*, 197) This statement reflects an antinomianism that contradicts both the words and spirit of Holy Scripture. As such, it begs questions and raises issues about the role played by rules in relationships.

Question one: As taught by Jesus, is any ingredient more important to a relationship than love, first between people and God, and second, among people with each other? Endorsing the Great Commandment and associating love with law, Jesus said:

> Thou shalt *love* the Lord thy God with all thy heart, and with all thy soul, and with all thy mind. This is *the first and great commandment*. And the second *is* like unto it, Thou shalt *love* thy neighbour as thyself. On these *two commandments* hang all *the law* and the prophets" (Emphasis Mine, Matthew 22:37-40, KJV).

There is no more essential ingredient to relationship than "love," for as Paul put it, love is "the greatest" (1 Corinthians 13:13).

Question two: Can you, dear reader, think of any element more necessary in the definition of *love* (relationship) than *laws* (rules)? No matter how *The Shack* spins it, relationships involve rules. Rules inform me where my rights end and another person's begin. The game of life must be played by the rules. As a deterrent to sinful behavior which can hurt the lives of others, rules become a necessary guide. They tell us what's right and what's wrong. Ever hear of the Ten Commandments (Exodus 20:1-17), or read the hundreds of other rules in the Bible?

Take adultery, for example. What if a man leaves his spouse and children to pursue a "relationship" with another woman? What arbitrates between those two competing relationships? They're both relationships, aren't they? Will laws? Will a judge? Or, do we simply endorse the moral chaos of self-indulgent "free love"? For the sake of arbitrating relationships, both the hierarchy and enforcement of law are needed.[5] While it is not that way amongst the members of the Holy Trinity in heaven, arbitration by rules is necessary for persons here on earth.

Like Jesus, the Apostle Paul therefore, combined law with the love, rules with relationship, writing:

> Owe no man any thing, but to *love one another*: for he that *loveth* another hath fulfilled the *law*. For this, <u>Thou shalt not</u> commit adultery, <u>Thou shalt not</u> kill, <u>Thou shalt not</u> steal, <u>Thou shalt not</u> bear false witness, <u>Thou shalt not</u> covet; and if there be any other *commandment*, it is briefly comprehended in this saying, namely, <u>Thou shalt</u> *love* thy neighbour as thyself. *Love* worketh no ill to his neighbour: therefore *love is* the fulfilling of the *law"* (Emphases Mine, Romans 13: 8-10).

When defining the love of earthy relationships, rules cannot be jettisoned. They are two sides of the same coin and cannot be separated. Both Jesus and Paul indicated that law (rules) complements love (relationships). Did not Jesus say that upon *loving* God and one's neighbor "hang all the *law* and the prophets"? But the sinful disposition residing in us ever threatens the relationships among us. Given sinful and selfish desires, and sometimes knowingly, we choose to indulge ourselves at a cost to others. When we break rules, we offend and hurt others, and in so doing, destroy relationships with them. When that happens, relationships need to be repaired. When marriages become broken by adultery, when the Seventh Commandment is violated, reconciliation needs to happen in order for the marriage to survive.[6] This is the real world in which we live, a world of broken relationships, and not an ethereal world pictured by a Thomas Kinkade painting. But the need for reconciliation exists not only between people, but also between individuals and God.

Sin Separates

The Christian underpinnings of *The Shack* make it necessary for the allegory to deal with fallen humanity's relationship with God, for as the prophet told Judah, "your iniquities have made a separation between you and your God" (Isaiah 59:2). For reason of sinning, the Bible depicts man to be estranged from God and living in a broken world. Thus *Papa* explains to Mack why things are the way they are when *she* says to him, "The world is broken because in Eden you abandoned relationship with us to assert your own independence." (*The Shack*,

146) Consistent with the allegory's antiauthoritarian and antinomian bent, *The Shack* defines sin as abandoning relationship.

But the Bible defines sin as breaking God's rules, for as John wrote, "sin is the transgression of the law" (1 John 3:4). The dynamic of sin is more than deserting relationship with God. In the allegory's explanation of the world's brokenness and the supposed importance of relationship over rules, a theological inconsistency arises. It is this: To explain his "sin-is-abandoning-relationship" theory, the author refers to the very Eden narrative in Genesis where God ordered Adam, "from the tree of the knowledge of good and evil you shall *not* eat" (Emphasis mine, Genesis 2:17). Ironically, by breaking the rule of God, Adam broke relationship with God. For doing so, God expelled Adam from Eden. So rules do have something to do with relationship. In fact, rules are tests of relationship! "Thou shalt not murder," it seems to me, would have been a good rule for Missy's killer to have obeyed. If he had, there would have been no *Great Sadness.*

Though for reason of God's grace, obedience to rules does not determine a person's relationship with Him (Ephesians 2:8-9), His rules do define what a relationship with Him looks like. Those who love God will not place other gods before Him. Those who love other persons will not covet their possessions. Anyone can say to someone else, "I love you!" Some men use the statement to manipulate and use women. They say it but do not mean it. So the greater question becomes, "<u>Do</u> you love me?" The Apostle Paul wrote repeatedly that "love <u>does</u> not" (Emphasis mine, 1 Corinthians 13:4-6). Love is more than saying. Love is doing and to that end, as the Ten Commandments indicate, rules profile how love behaves, what love does.

So the question becomes, after ruining our Eden by our sin, after having broken "relationship" with God, how can we reconciled to Him? Note: Though we need to be reconciled to God, God does not need to be reconciled to us. He has done nothing to offend us. But before dealing with our necessity to be reconciled to God, William Paul Young's position should be noted; that is, he believes in a universal reconciliation which finds basis in divine love eclipsing divine wrath, with the consequence that God becomes reconciled to the world.

Wayne Jacobsen, one of Young's collaborators and editors in writing *The Shack*, admits that universal reconciliation was part of the book's "earlier versions because of the author's partiality at that time to some aspects of what people call UR."[7] According to a professor and acquaintance of the author, "Paul's embrace of universal reconciliation . . . lies embedded in the book."[8] But just what is universal reconciliation?

In the words of one theologian, universal reconciliation,

> maintains that Christ's death accomplished its purpose in reconciling all humankind to God. The death of Christ made it possible for God to accept all humans, and he has done so. Consequently, whatever separation exists between a human and the benefits of God's grace is subjective in nature; it exists only in the human's mind.[9]

In short, universal reconciliation holds that without exception or reservation, all persons are saved for reason of Christ's atonement. The world needs to do nothing to be reconciled to God, for according to *Papa, she* is fully reconciled to the world.

While talking with Mack and crossing *her* arms on the table, *Papa* leans forward and says to him, "Honey, you asked me what Jesus did on the cross; so now listen to me carefully: through his death and resurrection, *I am now fully* reconciled to the world." (Emphasis mine, *The Shack*, 192) In a later conversation, *Papa* tells Mack, "In Jesus, *I have forgiven all humans* for their sins against me, but only some choose relationship." (Emphasis mine, *The Shack*, 225) Rightly, the allegory points to Jesus' cross as the centerpiece of reconciliation; but wrongly, on a number of counts, *Papa's* statements can be misleading.

God's State

First, God's *state* is not one of being reconciled to the world. In fact, God does not need to be reconciled to the world for He has never done anything to estrange Himself from the world. About the New Testament passages dealing with reconciliation between man and God, in his classic work *The Death of Christ*, James Denney commented:

> Where reconciliation is spoken of in St. Paul, the subject is always God, and the object is always man. The work of reconciling is one in which the initiative is taken by God, and the cost borne by Him; men are reconciled in the passive, or allow themselves to be

> reconciled, or receive reconciliation. *We never read that*
> *God has been reconciled.*[10]

Denney's statement contradicts *Papa's*.

To see whether Denney's observation is correct, we should notice three central New Testament passages that mention man's reconciliation to God (Romans 5:10; 2 Corinthians 5:18-21; Colossians 1:21, KJV). In each of these passages, God is the subject of reconciliation, and man is the object. In these passages, man is reconciled to God, and not the other way around. We quote:

> For if, when we were enemies, <u>we were reconciled to</u>
> <u>God</u> by the death of his Son, much more, being reconciled, we shall be saved by his life. (Emphasis Mine, Romans 5:10)

> And all things *are* of <u>God</u>, who hath <u>reconciled us</u> to himself by Jesus Christ, and hath given to us the ministry of reconciliation; To wit, that <u>God was in</u> <u>Christ, reconciling the world</u> unto himself, not imputing their trespasses unto them; and hath committed unto us the word of reconciliation. Now then we are ambassadors for Christ, as though God did beseech *you* by us: we pray *you* in Christ's stead, <u>be ye</u> <u>reconciled to God</u>. (Emphasis Mine, 2 Corinthians 5:18-20)

> <u>And you</u>, that were sometime alienated and enemies in *your* mind by wicked works, yet now <u>hath he reconciled</u> in the body of his flesh through death, to present you holy and unblameable and unreproveable in his sight. (Emphasis Mine, Colossians 1:21-22)

These Scriptures do not reveal that God has been reconciled to man. God possesses no "need" to be reconciled to sinners. While through the cross God reconciles sinners to Himself, it is not the other way around. In this light, the two adverbs which modify "reconciled" in *Papa's* statement are troubling.

The adverb "I am *now*" suggests there was a time when God was not and therefore personally needed to be reconciled to sinners.[11] The adverb describes the state of something in the present that was not the case in the past. But as has already been noted, the cross did not reconcile God to sinners, but rather, made it possible for sinners to be reconciled to God. From the divine perspective, the atonement made the world savable.

The second adverb, "I am now *fully*," implies that nothing else is needed for reconciliation to occur.[12] Papa's declaration makes it seem that, as far as God is concerned, reconciliation is a done deal—that peace between God and man has been secured when in fact it has not. Yes, on the basis of Jesus' atonement, God offers the "olive branch" of reconciliation to people, but it does not stand that they are automatically reconciled to God or are moved to accept His peace plan (i.e., the Gospel). As has been pointed out, there are people who refuse to believe the Gospel thereby short circuiting relationship with Him. Therefore, it cannot be rightfully stated that God is "*now fully* reconciled to the world."

Humanity's Standing

Second, the world's *standing* is not one of being *fully* reconciled to God. The "atonement" of Jesus forces nobody into "at-one-ment" with Him. Though the cross makes reconciliation with God accessible to man, it is not thereby consequent that all persons will receive the reconciliation He offers, for God does not coerce people into relationship with Him. He invites, but does not impose. Thus, after declaring others and himself to be "ambassadors for Christ," the Apostle asks, "as though God were entreating through us; *we beg you on behalf of Christ, be reconciled to God*" (Emphasis mine, 2 Corinthians 5:20).

If everybody stands "now fully" reconciled to God, then Paul's plea is unnecessary. But in the cross, God is simply saying to man, "These are the terms by which you may be reconciled to Me. *Now*, it's your move." Theologian Thomas Oden states that the completed work of the cross is an offer,

> to receive God's reconciling act. Until that occurs through repentance and faith, the sinner remains behaviorally unreconciled to God, even though God offers it already as a gift . . .[13]

But obviously, there is a sense in which, despite the cross, all persons do not receive God's pleading invitation to be at peace with Him. For whatever the reason, many persons ignore or refuse God's plea. They are unmoved. Resolutely, they follow their own spiritual agenda. For example, the agenda of some is *atheistic*. They mock the thought of God's existence. The agenda of others might be *hedonistic*. They love "feel-good" experiences more than God. Others are *narcissistic*. They love themselves more than God. Others are *materialistic* in life. They love things more than God. If any of these attitudes dictate our lifestyle, then Scripture declares "the love of the Father is not in" us (1 John 2:15). James states that, "whosoever therefore will be a friend of the world is the enemy of God" (James 4:4).

There are those who mock the gospel, who think of it as either foolishness or a scandal (1 Corinthians 1:23). Do such attitudes and responses evidence a state of being at peace with God? Without exception, all persons are not "fully" reconciled to God, for if they were, they would all be saved. So the question arises, how can someone be reconciled to God?

Justification and Reconciliation

Adolf Schlatter stated that because reconciliation is an aspect of justification, "reconciliation occurs by faith" (Romans 5:8).[14] Absent repentance for sin and faith in the Gospel, persons will remain un-reconciled to God forever (Romans 1:5; Hebrews 11:6). Though God extends the olive branch of peace to people, many refuse to accept the divinely initiated overture thereby imploding the whole reconciliation process. They refuse to accept God's peace plan. The sinful rebels remain at war with God. We turn now to address the theological implications of universalism—how UR affects other vital Christian teachings.

Universal Reconciliation: Theological Implications

Writing from the standpoint of being a one time "theological buddy" of Paul Young, James De Young notes that the "the most serious error is Paul's embrace of universal reconciliation which lies imbedded in the book."[15] When applied to Christianity, Universal Reconciliation (UR) behaves like a computer virus that first invades, and then infects the whole body of biblical truth. Contradicting distinctive Christian teachings, UR proposes a dialectic that changes biblical beliefs about God's love and justice, Jesus' atonement, heaven and hell, and the balance between divine sovereignty and human responsibility.

Divine Love and Justice

In the composite of His being, the loving God is interested in personal relationships (John 1:12). But at the same time, He remains holy and just (Isaiah 6:1-7; Genesis 18:25). At one and the same time, He is both separate from and near to His creation and

His creatures. At times, He even becomes angry with people (Ezekiel 16:26; 38:17-23).[16] After all, how should God feel about and respond to the crimes and injustices He sees perpetrated by one group or individual against others? Should He idly stand by and let the villains get away with it? If UR is true, then, yes. Love trumps anger and justice. But if UR is not true, the answer is, no. Sooner or later, in this life or the next, God will bring the bad guys to justice and punish them. This is the wrath of God. But in sync with a UR worldview, *The Shack* manifests aversion to the idea of divine wrath.

Alluding to a biblical statement in the book of James—by the way, biblical allusion can peddle spiritual delusion—the sensual *Sophia* tells Mack that Jesus and *Papa* chose the way of the cross, "For love." The "all-wise-Sophia" then explains to Mack, "He chose the way of the cross where mercy triumphs over justice because of love."[17] Rebuking Mack, who is role-playing Judge, she asks, "Would you instead prefer he'd chosen justice for everyone? Do you want justice, 'Dear Judge'?" (*The Shack*, 164-165) For salvation to be universal, God's love (mercy) must overrule God's justice (righteousness) thereby violating any sense of fair play.

When isolated from the rest of Scripture, and on the face of it, James' statement ("mercy triumphs over judgment," James 2:13b), might seem to support the contention that God's mercy will trump His justice in the end. But as the context shows (James 2:1-13), James is addressing the issue of equity between people, admonishing them to work out their relationships according to God's rules ("Thou shalt love thy neighbor as thyself . . . Do not commit adultery. . . Do not kill."). If they discriminate against the less fortunate around them, if they fail to love their fellows, then they can be certain of one thing: "judgment *will be* merciless to one who has shown no mercy" (James 2:13a, NASB). In other words, the first half of the verse affirms our accountability to God for how we treat others. Give no mercy in this life, receive no mercy in the next life (Compare Matthew 5:7.). On the other hand, the merciful will be exonerated, for in the last judgment "mercy triumphs over judgment" for them. Ironically, the first half of the verse affirms the opposite from what UR supposes the last half does; namely, that mercy does not override justice. Because God's being is balanced, His love does not diminish His justice (Galatians 5:21;

Revelation 20:10, 15; 21:8; 22:15). Yet one scene in the *The Shack*
suggests the opposite.

In a comfortable, schmoozing, and relational conversation
about the Canadian rock musician Bruce Cockburn, *Papa* says to
Mack, "Mackenzie, I have no favorites; I am just especially fond of
him." Mack then responds, "You seem to be especially fond of a
lot of people . . . Are there any who you are *not* especially fond of?"
After pensively contemplating the question, *Papa* responds, "Nope,
I haven't been able to find any. Guess that's jes' the way I is." (*The
Shack*, 118-119) Bingo! God is as "fond" of Nero, Adolf Hitler,
Joseph Stalin, and Saddam Hussein as He is of Jesus, or Mother
Theresa. It's all one big "circle of relationship" ("Kum Ba Ya"). As
Morris comments:

> The other religions of the world, in either ancient or
> modern times, lack a deep sense of the purity and
> holiness of God and of the ill desert of sin. It is
> thought unpalatable to man that God's holiness must
> be taken seriously in any attempt to solve the problem
> of reconciliation.[18]

Universalism necessitates imagining a God at variance from His
transparent self-disclosure in the Bible. So for reason of God's love
eclipsing divine wrath, *The Shack* jettisons the doctrine of Jesus'
penal and substitutionary atonement for sin.

Jesus' Cross and Sin

Theologian Wayne Grudem explains that the penal-
substitutionary atonement of Christ "has been the orthodox
understanding of the atonement . . . in contrast to *other views that
attempt to explain the atonement apart from the idea of the wrath of God* or
payment of the penalty for sin."[19] Because in *The Shack's* view
divine love supersedes divine wrath, we would expect to find
indication in the book that Jesus did not die as our representative
to provide a penal-substitutionary atonement for sin. And this we
find.

No Punishment—Oh Really?

In a poignant moment with "deep sadness in her eyes,"
Papa tells Mack":

> I am not who you think I am, Mackenzie. I don't need
> to punish people for sin. Sin is its own punishment,

> devouring you from the inside. It is not my purpose to
> punish it; it's my joy to cure it. (*The Shack*, 119-120)

Thus, a Christian reader is left groping to explain why Jesus died. We need to understand the relationship of human sin to divine punishment.

Though Paul Young vaguely infers that the atonement might be substitutionary (*The Shack*, 162), he does not, for reason of love eclipsing wrath, and for reason of Papa's co-crucifixion with Jesus, present it as the payment of a penalty for sin (Remember *Papa* said: "I don't need to punish people for sin."). The issue is not whether God *needs* to punish people for sin. After all, who are we to tell God what His needs are, or are not? (See Acts 17:25.) The issue is whether God *does* punish sin, and according to the Bible, He *has* punished, *still* punishes, and *will* punish sin (Compare Genesis 6:5-7; Romans 1:24-32; Revelation 21:8, 27; 22:15.).

The Bible tells us that physical death is God's continuing punishment for sin. Though we may deny we're sinners, we cannot claim exemption from death. The Apostle Paul wrote, "Therefore, just as through one man sin entered into the world, and death through sin, and so death spread to all men, because all sinned" (Romans 5:12; Compare Genesis 2:16-17.). So if God possesses no "need" to punish people for sin, then why not abolish death *now*? But excepting the generation of the translation (1 Corinthians 15:50-56), we are all destined to die. As a pundit put it, "The statistics on death are overwhelming. One out of one person dies!" Death happens. I know, for as a pastor, I've officiated at hundreds of funerals. So about the inference that God doesn't punish sin, let's get real. If He still punishes sin in time, how can we be sure He won't punish sin in eternity? We can't and this fact brings us to consider the death of Jesus.

Jesus' Penal-Substitutionary Atonement

Though men dispute the reason for Jesus' death, and whether or not He was raised from the dead, they do not dispute that He died. That's history. He lived. He died. In light of death's cause, that it remains a continuing punishment for sin, the begging question becomes—why did Jesus die? Did He die to be punished for His own sins? If so, then He was just another sinner like the rest of us because "the wages of sin is death" (Romans 6:23). But the Scriptures declare Him to be sinless (Hebrews 4:15; 1 Peter

1:19). Thus, did He, as opposed to the forbidding idea that He died
for His own sins, vicariously die as the penal substitute for the sins
of others? The Scriptures declare this to be the reason Christ
suffered and died (Isaiah 53:4-6; 2 Corinthians 5:21). In fact, that's
why Jesus said He would die (Mark 10:45) Now either Jesus
deserved to die for His own sin(s), or He died for the sins of
others. As Donald Macleod summarizes:

> People speak with horror of 'the penal theory of the
> atonement'. But what happened to Christ on the cross?
> He died. And what is death? It is the penalty for sin! . . .
> On that cross He was dealt with as sin deserved. The
> glory of it is, it wasn't His own sin. It was our sin. He
> bore the sin of the world (John 1:29).[20]

As with other world religions, and believing that people
want a relationship with God,[21] universal salvation rejects the idea
that sin is a personal offense against God that deserves punishment
(Contra Psalm 51:1-4; Romans 3:21-26; 1 John 2:2; 4:10.).
Therefore, any thought of a penal substitutionary atonement lies
beneath the dignity of the idol god manufactured by the "touchy-
touchy-feely-feely" crowd of contemporary Christians. The author
of *The Shack* is on record denying this view of the atonement. In an
interview Paul Young confessed to the interviewer, "No . . . I am
not a penal substitution . . . reformation . . . point of view."[22]

Jesus' Death Provides an Inspiring Example

If all persons are saved (i.e., universally reconciled), then
the question arises, "Why did God's Son—the Lamb—die on the
cross?" Regarding universalism and Christ's atonement, Robertson
McQuilken summarizes the dilemma:

> For if all sin will ultimately be overlooked by a gracious
> deity, Christ never should have died. It was not only
> unnecessary, it was surely the greatest error in history . .
> . Universalism . . . demands a view of the death of
> Christ as having some purpose other than as an
> atonement for sin.[23]

In universalism's salvific scheme it must be concluded that Jesus
died for a reason other than that we might be forgiven for our sins.

Beginning with Abelard (1079-1142), liberal Christianity
proposes that Jesus died to provide mankind with an inspiring and

sacrificial example.[24] One theologian frames the liberal theory of the atonement as follows: "If there is anything liberal theology is agreed upon it is that the frequent biblical references to God's wrath (anger, displeasure, indignation, rage, vengeance) must be interpreted down to mean something like frustrated love."[25] And that is exactly as *The Shack* would have it—*Papa's* love is frustrated because her children do not seek "relationship" with her. But in the end, she will impose her universal love upon them anyway.

As I see it, the atonement theory of *The Shack* seems to be that Jesus died to inspire people to become more selfless as they seek "relationship" with God and each other. (*The Shack*, 225) Though Jesus' death does provide us with a selfless example (John 15:13), the implications of His atonement are far more profound.

In a Universal Reconciliation scheme of redemption, divine wrath needs to be toned down. This may explain why *The Shack* pictures *Papa* as having been co-crucified with Jesus. (*The Shack*, 95, 102, 107, 222) As evidenced by the Jesus-like scars on her wrists, *Papa* had magnanimously borne her own wrath. This is the ancient heresy of modalism in which the three members of the Trinity are so fused in their relationship that any personal distinction between them is lost. Perhaps *Papa* even atoned for her sins. Who knows? But in that *Papa* was crucified *with Jesus*, it cannot be held that Christ suffered and died alone as man's penal-substitute.[26] (*The Shack*, 96) In a supreme exhibition of love, *Papa* helped take the hit.

Heaven and Hell

According to the worldview of *The Shack*, hell cannot exist because evil, however it may be perceived, is not real. It's a mirage. *Sarayu* (the Holy Spirit) tells Mack, "Both evil and darkness can only be understood in relation to Light and Good; they (i.e., 'evil and darkness') do not have any actual existence." (*The Shack*, 136) The logic of universalism might be constructed like this:

> The omni-present God of light is omni-benevolent toward all people.
> Hell would be dark, malevolent, and restricted place for some people.
> Therefore, assuming God's omni-presence and omni-benevolence, hell can't exist.

Thus, as a place of "eternal punishment" and "outer darkness" (Matthew 8:12; 22:13; 25:30, 46), universalism denies the existence of hell. God is "fond" of everyone. Universal Reconciliation cannot allow for a place where men are eternally separated from God, where any hope for "relationship" with God would be devastated.[27] However metaphorical it might be, I think of the sign over the inferno in Dante's *Divine Comedy*, "All hope abandon ye who enter here." Hope can't happen in hell.

Divine Sovereignty and Human Responsibility

It can also be charged that UR is fatalistic. Freedom of choice is violated to such a degree that even atheists are forced to spend eternity with a person they do not like in a place where they did not want to go—with God in heaven. There are fools who mutter in their hearts, "No God" (Psalm 14:1; 53:1). Sadly, the Bible describes some people as "haters of God" (Romans 1:30). Are we to project those individuals, who possessed deep and residual animus toward God in this life and who spent the whole of their lives despising and denying Him, will derive one moment's pleasure from being in the presence of the One whom in their heart of hearts they continue to loathe? Will God grab these despisers and deniers by the nape of their necks and drag them "kicking and screaming" into heaven? Thus, C.S. Lewis wrote:

> There are only two kinds of people in the end: those who say to God, 'Thy will be done,' and those to whom God says, in the end, '*Thy* will be done.' All that are in Hell, choose it. Without that self-choice there could be no Hell.[28]

Similarly, Alister McGrath also remarks: "Universalism perverts the gospel of the love of God into an obscene scene of theological rape quite unworthy of the God whom we encounter in the face of Jesus Christ."[29]

Conclusion

Absent faith in and acceptance of the truth, the differences between God and sinners are irreconcilable. Exhibiting that people can and do reject "relationship" with God, even after extensive pleading to be reconciled, Jesus lamented over the ancient Jewish nation, "O Jerusalem, Jerusalem, *thou* that killest the prophets, and stonest them which are sent unto thee, how often would I have gathered thy children together, even as a hen gathereth her chickens under *her* wings, and *ye would not!"* (Emphasis Mine, Matthew 23:37, KJV). If any person refuses relationship based upon the terms of the Gospel, they will remain un-reconciled to God . . . forever. But Christian believers have been reconciled and possess an eternal relationship with God through faith in the penal and substitutionary blood atonement of the Lord Jesus Christ. According to the Scriptures, "Christ died for our sins" (1 Corinthians 15:3). As a hymn writer states:

> Bearing shame and scoffing rude,
> In my place condemned He stood—
> Sealed my pardon with His blood:
> Hallelujah! what a Savior!

> Guilty, vile and helpless we,
> Spotless Lamb of God was He;
> Full atonement! Can it be?
> Hallelujah! what a Savior![30]

ENDNOTES

[1] UR is the belief that every person who has ever lived is, or will be, either before or after death, reconciled to God. Historically, universal reconciliation leads to Unitarianism which denies the biblical Trinity. After all, if God saves all persons, who needs Christ and His atonement on the cross, or application of salvation to the human soul by the Holy Spirit?

[2] R.E.O. White, "Reconciliation," *The Concise Evangelical Dictionary of Theology*, Edited by Walter A. Elwell, Abridged by Peter Toon (Grand Rapids: Baker Book House, 1991) 420. Morris determined that, "The basic idea of reconciliation is that of making peace after a quarrel, or bridging over an enmity." See Leon Morris, *The Cross in the New Testament* (Grand Rapids: William B. Eerdmans Publishing Company, 1965) 250.

[3] White, "Reconciliation," 421.

[4] Over forty times *The Shack* uses the word "relationship(s)." Indeed, though perhaps overdrawn, exaggerated, and even at points, profaned, one of the strengths of the story is its emphasis on relationship.

[5] Rules in Scripture exhibit God's righteousness (i.e., justice), and are an essential aspect of relationships. Being sourced in His absolute authority and infinite wisdom, God's law(s) orients mankind as to the good or evil of behaviors which either help or hurt others. Inherent to real love is right law.

God's rules declare which behaviors best benefit how people should relate to Him and to each other. His guidelines objectify correct spirituality and morality. Because God is right, God is Righteous. Thus,

God's righteousness might be understood like this: Out of His love and concern for the relational wellbeing of humanity—God does desire that people live in peace and harmony with one another—He, after the eternal counsel of His infinite wisdom, designed rules to promote harmony amongst humanity. God communicates His rules in the Bible (e.g., the Ten Commandments). Because He is righteous, God keeps His rules. He conforms to His own standards. Because He is absolutely righteous and just, one day God will bring humanity into account for how they obeyed the laws of love. He will judge the world. He will enforce the rules. "God *is* a just judge, and God is angry *with the wicked* every day" (Psalm 7:11; See Romans 2:5-16).

[6] On this point, we must note how Scripture employs the images of adultery or harlotry to picture Israel's breaking "relationship" with God (See Isaiah 1:21; Jeremiah 3:1; 23:10; Ezekiel 16:15-63; James 4:4.). In both its sexual and spiritual dimensions, adultery signals the breaking of relationship, and that is why God said, "Thou shalt not commit adultery" (Exodus 20:15). So for violating the Seventh Commandment, Jehovah divorced Israel (Jeremiah 3:8).

[7] Wayne Jacobsen, "Is *The Shack* Heresy? *LifeStream Blog,* (http://lifestream.org/blog/2008/03/04/is-the-shack-heresy/ Windblownmedia. Com).

[8] An acquaintance of Paul Young, a "theological buddy," has written an extended essay that tracks *The Shack's* universalism. See James B. De Young, *At the Back of the Shack a Torrent of Universalism* (Damascus, Oregon: Revised May 2008, 39 pages). Professor De Young's essay can be downloaded online in a PDF format at (http:// theshackreview.com/content/ReviewofTheShack.pdf). Like Jacobsen in the preceding quote, De Young states, "About four years ago Paul embraced universal reconciliation, and strongly defended his decision" (p. 5).

[9] Millard J. Erickson, *Christian Theology,* Second Edition (Grand Rapids: Baker Books, 1998) 1027.

[10] Emphasis Mine, James Denney, *The Death of Christ* (Minneapolis: Klock & Klock Christian Publishers, Inc., 1982 Reprint) 103. Morris also states: "It is interesting to notice that no New Testament passage speaks of Christ reconciling God to man. Always the stress is on man being reconciled. . . . It is man's sin which has caused the enmity." See Leon L. Morris, "Reconciliation," *The New Bible Dictionary*, J.D. Douglas, Organizing Editor (Grand Rapids: Wm. B. Eerdmans Publishing Co., 1962) 1077. Further, of the eleven New Testament mentions of reconciliation, "in every instance man is said to be reconciled to God." See John F. Walvoord, *Jesus Christ Our Lord* (Chicago: Moody Press, 1969) 179.

[11] As dictionaries define the word, "now" means "at this time or moment . . . nowadays." See *The Random House College Dictionary*, Revised, Laurence Urdang, Editor in Chief (New York: Random House, 1988) 911.

[12] The word means "containing all that can be held; filled to the utmost capacity; . . . complete; entire." See Ibid. 534.

[13] Thomas C. Oden, *The Word of Life, Systematic Theology: Volume Two* (Peabody, Massachusetts: Prince Press, 1989) 356.

[14] Adolf Schlatter, *The Theology of the Apostles*, Translated by Andreas J. Köstenberger (Grand Rapids: Baker Books, 1999) 246.

[15] De Young, *Back of the Shack*, 3. De Young notes that, "The greatest doctrinal distortion in the book is Paul's assumption of universal reconciliation" (p.3), and that the book's storyline has "universal reconciliation at its base." (p.4)

[16] "A study of the concordance will show that there are *more* references in Scripture to the anger, fury, and wrath of God, than there are to His love and tenderness." See Arthur W. Pink, *The Attributes of God* (Grand Rapids: Baker Book House, 1975) 82. After describing the fear of a little boy who, because of intimidating scenes recorded in the Old Testament, thought of Jehovah as a "dirty bully," a liberal preacher explained: "We have long since rejected a conception of reconciliation associated historically with the idea of a Deity that is loathsome. God, for us, cannot be thought of as angry . . . who because of Adam's sin must have his Shylockian (i.e., ruthless money-lending) pound of flesh." See G. Bromley Oxnam, *Preaching in a Revolutionary Age* (Freeport, New York: Books for Libraries Series, 1971) 79. The book comprises the Lyman Beecher lectures on preaching at Yale Divinity School, 1943-44.

[17] The allusion is to James 2:13, where the second half of the verse states, "mercy triumphs over judgment" (NASB).

[18] Morris, *The Cross*, 250-251.

[19] Emphasis Mine, Wayne Grudem, *Systematic Theology* (Grand Rapids: Zondervan Publishing House, 1994) 579.

[20] Donald Macleod, *A Faith to Live By, Understanding Christian Doctrine* (Great Britain: Christian Focus Publications, 2002) 151.

[21] Contra Romans 3:11 which says, "there is none that seeketh after God."

[22] *More Books and Things . . .* , March 11, 2009, Transcript of Interview on Radio Station KAYP (http:// morebooksandthings. blogspot.com/2009/03/transcript-of-interview.html). Four months before this interview and from reading *The Shack*, I concluded that Young did not, for reason of his view that divine love eclipses divine wrath, believe in the penal substitutionary atonement. My impression is documented in a consecutive three part series of articles on Universal

Reconciliation which appeared on the *Herescope* blog on the dates, October 21, 24, and 31, 2008 (http://herescope.blogspot.com/2008/10/universal-reconciliation.html) and are updated in this chapter.

[23] Robertson McQuilken, *The Great Omission, A Biblical Basis for World Evangelism* (Waynesboro, Georgia: Authentic Media, 2002) 41.

[24] Grounds summarized that Abelard's "view of our Lord's passion, exhibiting the great love of God, so frees us from the fear of wrath that we may serve him in love." He notes that by subordinating "everything to the controlling idea that the cross" is the demonstration of God's love, man's love for God is "almost automatically" drawn out in return. Abelard's theory fits the meaning of the atonement described in *The Shack*. See Vernon C. Grounds, "Atonement," *Baker's Dictionary of Theology*, Everett F. Harrison, Editor-in-Chief (Grand Rapids: Baker Book House, 1960) 73.

[25] Robert Duncan Culver, *Systematic Theology* (Great Britain: Christian Focus Publications, Ltd., 2005) 553.

[26] *Papa* tells Mack, "Don't ever think that what my son chose to do didn't cost us dearly. Love always leaves a significant mark . . . We were there *together*." (*The Shack*, 96) This statement is made in spite of the fact of Jesus' cry, "Eli, Eli, lama sabachthani? that is to say, My God, my God, why hast thou forsaken me?" (Matthew 27:46).

[27] Brian D. McLaren disdains "violence and war" writing that it "is one of the reasons many of us have become critical in recent years of popular American eschatology in general, and conventional views of hell in particular." See *Everything Must Change* (Nashville: Thomas Nelson, 2007) 144. Nobody I know likes violence and war. I don't. Yet the testaments, both Old and New, from beginning to end, contain it. Is the eschatology, McLaren and others are critical of, American, or biblical? Remember: America did not hatch the Bible.

[28] C.S. Lewis, *The Great Divorce, The Best of C.S. Lewis* (New York: Christianity Today, Inc., 1969) 156. I thank Dr. De Young for drawing my attention to Lewis' quote.

[29] Alister McGrath, *Justification by Faith* (Grand Rapids: Zondervan Publishing House, 1988) 106. Though he is an Arminian within the camp of open theism, Clark Pinnock states: "Universalism is not a viable position because of the gift of human freedom." See William Crockett, General Editor, *Four Views on Hell* (Grand Rapids: Zondervan Publishing House, 1996) 128.

[30] Philip P. Bliss, "Hallelujah, What a Savior!" *The Celebration Hymnal* (Dallas: Word/Integrity, 1997) 311.

ON THE ROCKS IN *THE SHACK*
Spiritual Adultery and Ruined Relationships

> Have you seen what faithless Israel did? She went
> up on every high hill and under every green tree,
> and she was a harlot there. . . . And I saw that for
> all the adulteries of faithless Israel, I had sent her
> away and given her a writ of divorce, yet her
> treacherous sister Judah did not fear; but she went
> and was a harlot also. (Jeremiah 3:6, 8, NASB)

In his chapter "A Breakfast of Champions" (By the way, I
like *WHEATIES* too!), *The Shack's* author, Paul Young, places
these words in the mouth of the Holy Spirit, *Sarayu*, as she
addresses Mack, the allegory's main character:

> Mackenzie, we have no concept of final authority
> among us, only unity. We are in a *circle* of relationship,
> not a chain of command or 'great chain of being' as
> your ancestors termed it. What you are seeing here is
> relationship without any overlay of power. (*The Shack*,
> 122)

The Shack is big on relationships. Forty-odd times the
author employs the word "relationship(s)." Like any existentialist,
the author takes liberty to reinvent "the relationships between
people and God."[1] Though at times profaned, one of the allegory's
strengths is the emphasis it places upon "relationship" among and
between the imaginary members of the trinity and Mack.

"Relationship" becomes most evident when "Papa" (a.k.a.
"Elousia," the black goddess) enfolded Mack—haunted by his
Great Sadness—into his/her arms and gently invited him to "Let it
all out." (*The Shack*, 226) In this poignant moment of emotional
catharsis, the story records that Mack, "closed his eyes as the tears
poured out . . . He wept until he had cried out all the darkness, all
the longing and all the loss, until there was nothing left." Thus, by
his "relationship" to the feminine-divine, Mack is restored to
emotional wholeness, something his temperamental and churlish
earthly father would have been incapable of helping him with, and
by implication, any purely heavenly Father.

This may explain why Paul Young paints God in the image of the feminine-divine. He thinks the image of a mother god can offer succor and comfort to humanity in ways of which God the Father is incapable, at least according to how the author projects a father image to be. But by linking emotional healing to feminine divinity, Young appears to have borrowed from a pagan storyline. But before addressing the link between goddess-ism and paganism, the masculinity of God as presented in Scripture deserves attention.

God "Is" Masculine

In a little book, *The Language of Canaan and the Grammar of Feminism*, Vernard Eller noted that, "the God/man relationship is to be understood primarily under three figures—each of which castes God in a clearly masculine role."[2] Those three metaphors are "(a) husband and wife (or lover and beloved); (b) father and child (normally 'children' or 'son'); and (c) king and people . . ."[3] In these figures Eller states, "God is masculine—and must be for the figure to work."[4] Again, in the divine human relationship, humanity assumes the feminine role "to put it in a way that is linguistically maddening and yet biblically true."[5] This contradicts the dominantly feminine manner in which Young presents God.

As the Bible pictures God as masculine and His people as feminine, let's look at the biblical metaphor of "husband and wife," the "overlay of power" attendant thereto, and explore how any role-reversal might alter a person's relationship to God.

Israel's Husband

In the Old Testament, Israel is known as the "wife of Jehovah," and in the New Testament the church as the "bride of Christ." Intimating that He was Husband to that nation when they broke covenant with Him, the Lord predicted His relationship with Judah would be restored.

> Behold, the days come, saith the Lord, that I will make a new covenant with the house of Israel, and with the house of Judah: Not according to the covenant that I made with their fathers in the day *that* I took them by the hand to bring them out of the land of Egypt; which my covenant they brake, although *I was an husband unto them*, saith the Lord" (Emphasis mine, Jeremiah 31:31-32, KJV).

Jeremiah pictures the relationship between God and the nation as that of Yahweh being the husband and Israel being His wife.[6]

The Church's Groom

Again, Jesus told a story about a wedding in waiting. He likened Himself as the Groom. He compared the people for whom He was coming to be His Bride—a coming that, though announced and expected, was going to be abrupt and surprising (Matthew 25:1-13). The Apostle Paul develops this marriage metaphor when, after setting forth the guidelines for intimacy in marriage, he said, "This mystery is great; but I am speaking with reference to Christ and the church" (Ephesians 5:32).

Thus, "husband" is a chief metaphor by which God explains His relationship to His people. The figure of marriage connotes the most intimate of "relationships"—the former involving Israel being the Lord's *partner*, and the later the church being His *promised*. The marriage figure is richly endowed with the image of the divine masculine (initiation, wooer) and the human feminine (response, wooed).[7] Such is the nature of divine grace. To invert the relationship creates a spiritual climate in which people initiate thereby creating their own gods and goddesses (idolatry), and make their own rules (legalism) by which they, because of their actions, expect to control God and cause Him to react favorably to them.[8] People become manipulators instead of worshippers.[9]

Femininity and the Trinity

Can the creation of a feminine-divine image as pictured in *The Shack* impede, even damage, the relational-potential between people and God, something polar opposite from what readers testify the book has done for them?[10] Can this happen when the story invites people into a surreal-spiritual world? Yes it can, for that is how imagination and idolatry relate to each other. But you might be asking, how? We would answer: By projecting femininity to the Trinity in a role-reversal that perverts what the Bible depicts the divine-human relationship to be.

Eller comments upon the biblical relationship between God and His people: "It is not wide the mark to say that, in Yahwism, the human race plays the role that goddesses play in the religions of dual-gendered deity."[11] He continues to say:

> This means that the biblical faith has built into it a much higher anthropology than is possible to any the pagan faiths—and let it be said, an anthropology that not only fully *includes* women but actually is *biased toward* the feminine. Consequently, we ought to be very

> cautious about falling for the temptation our biblical
> predecessors so valiantly resisted, namely, moving the
> feminine principle into the godhead and thus
> jeopardizing the great anthropological (and feminist)
> advantage scripture had already given us.[12]

The above quotation may need clarification on one point;
that goddess-ism is something "our biblical predecessors . . .
valiantly resisted."[13] The fact of the matter is—the vast majority did
not valiantly resist the temptation posed by female idols. Only a
remnant did (1 Kings 19:18; Romans 11:4-5). The Old Testament is
littered with examples of idolism in which worshippers projected
their gods to be goddesses. The Lord tells Jeremiah that, "The
children gather wood, and the fathers kindle the fire, and the
women knead dough to make cakes for the queen of heaven; and
they pour out libations to other gods in order to spite Me"
(Jeremiah 7:18, NASB). The name "queen of heaven" may refer an
aggregate of feminine deities extant in the ancient world—Isis
(Egyptian), Astarte (Phoenician), Ishtar (Assyrian and Babylonian),
Ashtoreth (Canaanite), Anat (Canaanite), and others. The
implication of such a relational role-reversal lies at the base of
demonic experiences, idolatrous practices, and false religion.

"Goddess-ism" in Ancient Israel

Though feminine idols permeated the religions of ancient
civilizations, and though its ideology may have secretly simmered
amidst the Israelites since their Egyptian captivity (Ezekiel 20:7-8),
goddess-ism seems to have gone public in Israel when introduced
by King Solomon. In an abrupt turnabout, the same king who had
constructed and dedicated the Temple that would house Yahweh's
glorious presence (1 Kings 6:1-38; 8:1-9:9), built worship centers
"before Jerusalem" to house, among others, images to the Sidonian
goddess Ashtoreth (1 Kings 11:1-8; 2 Kings 23:13). In his later life,
and for reason of possessing hundreds of wives and concubines,
Solomon's sexual desires turned his heart unto other gods and
goddesses. The king's sensuality led him into idolatry.

More than a Metaphor

Solomon's personal involvement with and public initiation
of idolatry at the end of his reign influenced Israel's and Judah's
spirituality for generations to come. The common biblical
description of Israel playing the harlot with the pagan (i.e., earthly)
idol-gods of the surrounding nations is more than a metaphor.[14]

Ritual Prostitution

As religion, the feminine goddess *Asherah* (or, Ashtoreth) was fully a part of Baal worship, she being the female consort of Baal.[15] This male-female divinity (i.e., Baal-Asherah) typifies the pagan idolatry where, as one study Bible notes, the "deities symbolized generative power, [and] their worship involved prostitution."[16]

As ritual, the intent behind religious prostitution was perhaps threefold: one, that worshippers could derive pleasure as they indulged their selfish lusts; two, that by engaging in the primal act by which the continuum of life is perpetuated, they could, in acts of imitative magic, somehow stimulate "the womb of mother earth" to open up thereby increasing the fertility of their flocks and crops; and three, that they could, for reason of ecstasy derived from the sexual liaison with a body representing a god or goddess, experience their personality, however fleetingly, become mystically fused with the divine.[17]

Thus, ritual prostitution involving males and females became a common occurrence at the many high places constructed "before Jerusalem" and throughout the nation (Jeremiah 3:6).[18] At this juncture, we should note a call from some that, in advocating New Age/New Spirituality, "We must allow ourselves whatever time it takes to reestablish the consciousness of the Sacred Prostitute."[19]

In spite of the outward repression of idolatry by reforms like those initiated by the youthful King Josiah (*circa* 622 B.C., 2 Chronicles 34:1-7), it has been noted that the idolatrous cancer "was deep and flourished quickly again after a shallow revival."[20] Not even the Babylonian Captivity would cure the nation of its fascination for and playing the harlot with the imagined gods and goddesses of the surrounding nations. In fact, the solution to this spiritual pollution awaits the coming of the One who will cure Israel and the world of spiritual harlotry forever (Zechariah 12:10; 13:2; See Micah 4:1-2.).

Obviously, *when* the image of God is changed into gods and goddesses (Romans 1:23), *when* poly-gendering generates polytheism, *when* the sacred-sexual on earth is believed to mirror the sacred-sexual in heaven (As above, so below.),[21] *when* sacred prostitutes become representative incarnations of the gods and goddesses, and *when* sex becomes a sacrament linking of the human to the divine, the dynamic of "relationship" with God changes.[22] Sensuality controls spirituality, and divine mystery is reduced to vulgar lust (See Leviticus 18:1-19:4; 1 Peter 1:15).

Evangelicals: Emergent and Erotic

Believing in the wholeness and sacredness of matter and energy (i.e., the monistic and pantheistic theory that God is all, and all is God), New Ageism views that sexuality complements spirituality. Sexual people are spiritual people, and sexual experiences are spiritual experiences. Sex facilitates persons getting in touch with the mystical dynamic and rhythm of life. Being one of the most vibrant experiences life offers, it is not therefore surprising that avant-garde religionists should attempt to combine sex and spirituality. One New Age author states:

> Sexual ecstasy can transport us into union with the sacred Other, whether soul, God, human beloved, or nature. Uninhibited sexual opening powerfully alters consciousness . . .[23]

In a similar vein, the stunning statement of a radical Anglican priest has been noted: "Sex is the spirituality that reveals the sacramental richness of matter."[24]

"Sex God"

Though he makes some legitimate observations in his book *Sex God, Exploring the Endless Connections between Sexuality and Spirituality*, like a New Age teacher, Emergent Church Pastor Rob Bell connects sexuality and spirituality. Though disclaiming that men and women are, or possess the potential to become, gods, Bell does state that,

> in some distinct, intentional way, something of God has been placed in them. We reflect what God is like and who God is. A divine spark resides in every single human being."[25]

To what does the "divine spark" refer? Does the "spark" refer to the soul-spirit of a person, or to sex?

To answer the questions, it must be noted that in his book Bell later stated, "Sex carries within it the power of Life . . . Something divine."[26] We should note how like New Age teacher Neale Donald Walsch, Bell spells *life* with a capital "L" and *creator* with lower case "c,"[27] and how like Eckhart Tolle, Bell views sex as "divine."[28] In spelling *life* with a capital "L" and calling *sex* "divine," is the hip Bell attempting to "Christianize" the sexuality of New Age spirituality? It appears so.

In that Bell *calls* sex "divine," *states* that our sexuality reflects "what God is like and who God is," and *modifies* God with the attributive adjective "sex" in the title of his book, he suggests that sexuality helps define God, and that sexuality is something God possesses in common with His creatures. But calling sex divine introduces eroticism into the nature of God, which becomes an interesting make-over for God, especially in light of the fact that eroticism was an essential component of the goddess-ism endemic to the ancient and pagan Near Eastern religions.[29]

Thus, one must question whether Bell's sex construct elevates or degrades the image of God in man, and whether it affirms or denies the transcendence and separateness of the Creator from His creation. I myself look at it like this: If it degrades God, then it degrades man. In pagan belief, sex is the spark that ignites and perpetuates life with a capital "L" and taps into energy with a capital "E." So if it is divine, why not spell sex with a capital "S"?[30] But I shudder to think of the perversity that can result from thinking that sex and God belong to the same cosmic and monistic whole—as below, so above.

Song of Solomon

Those who connect sexuality to spirituality think they find precedent for doing so in the biblical book, *Song of Solomon.* Though no evangelical, Matthew Fox presupposes that Christ and the universe are co-extensive. Together, they form a cosmic Christ.[31] In his pantheistic monism, Fox relates sexuality to the Creation. He states:

> the Cosmic Christ is encountered in human love and sexuality. Sexuality is revealed in a living cosmology as still one other theophany, one other transfiguration experience.[32]

To him as well as other New Age/New Spiritualists, sexuality serves to enhance one's sense of feeling spiritually connected to the cosmos.

Thus, Fox writes of a Christ who is present in, with, and around sex. After treating human sexuality in the biblical book *Song of Solomon*, Fox writes that, "Play lies at the essence of all sexuality re-visioned in light of a Cosmic Christ paradigm."[33] Likewise, in his book, *Life with God*, well-known contemplative author Richard Foster states that, "the luscious imagery of Song of Solomon has forever linked the spiritual and the erotic with exquisite unity."[34] New Calvinist Pastor Mark Driscoll also makes extensive use of *Song of Solomon* when he dispenses his often uncouth "sexpertise."[35]

However, *Song of Solomon* does not describe a love affair between people and God. The love scenes are earthbound. The book depicts the ideal, wholesome, and faithful courtship and marriage between two earthly lovers. As such, the *Song* may be understood "as a series of six major poems . . . put together in a sequence that builds from anticipation (Poems I-II) to consummation (Poem III) to aftermath (Poems IV-VI)."[36] Old Testament scholar David Hubbard suggested that this understanding "shies away from any *allegorical* handling of the text, since it [the text] contains no clue as to hidden or spiritual meanings . . . ." He concludes that, "the New Testament, which does not quote or refer to it, gives no support to attempts to spiritualize the book."[37] Those who connect sexuality to spirituality for reason of *Song of Solomon* do so in spite of the fact that the book contains no mention of God's name.[38]

Nevertheless, desperate to find some analogical reason or biblical authority to combine sensuality and spirituality, the New Spiritualists allegorize the *Song* to describe the sensuality between God and His lovers. But since the days of Origen (*circa* 185-254) the allegorical method of interpretation has led to many wild and fanciful scenarios. Using *Song of Solomon* to infer support for the idea of "sacred sex" is just such a fancy.

"Goddess-ism" in The Shack

In *The Shack's* relaxed, give-and-take, and schmoozing atmosphere created by Young, the author injects sensuality into Mack's relationship with the feminine-divine. On two separate occasions—once with the sensual *Sophia* (the personification of *Papa's* Wisdom), and then later with *Sarayu* (the Holy Spirit)—Mack seemingly experienced *kundalini*–like ecstasy.

According to Yoga teaching, *kundalini* describes a mystical experience or orgasm of soul when a zap of energy enters the body. This experience, which can happen spontaneously, is named *kundalini* (*Sanskrit* for "snake" or "serpent power"; named as such because of the Hindu belief that like a "sleeping serpent," it lies coiled within the body ready to strike at any moment. Might this bear similarity to Genesis 3:1?). When the energy awakens the serpent, wham . . .! This powerful but transient moment of psycho-spiritual arousal is defined to include, "physical sensations . . . clairaudience, visions, brilliant lights . . . ecstasy, bliss, and transcendence of self."[39]

Kundalini and Chakras

Yoga teaches that in the human body there are, "vortices that penetrate the body and the body's aura, through which various energies, including the universal life force, are received, transformed, and distributed."[40] The entry points for the energy are called *chakras*. It is believed that there are seven such points (*chakras*) where the energy enters. They include:

> The root (*muladhara*) [which] is located at the base of the spine and is the seat of *kundalini* . . .; the sacral (*svadhisthana*) [which] lies near the genitals and governs sexuality . . .; [and] the crown (*sahasrara*) [which] whirls just above the top of the head.[41]

With this description in mind, let's look at two instances in *The Shack* to see if Mack, the novel's main character, experienced something like *kundalini*.

Upon hearing the sensual *Sophia* ask him, during a séance-like journey into the darkness, "Do you understand why you're here?" the story records:

> Mack could almost feel her words (Clairaudience) rain down on his head first (The 7th chakra?) and melt into his spine (The 1st chakra?), sending delicious tingles everywhere (The 2nd chakra?). He shivered (Physical sensations) and decided that he never wanted to speak again (Self-transcendence). He only wanted her to talk (Bliss) . . . (Parenthetical notes, questions, and associations mine, *The Shack*, 153)

Or consider the moment when *Sarayu*, in affirming her constant presence with Mack, told him, "I am always with you; sometimes I want you to be aware in a special way—more intentional." Then Young records that Mack, "distinctly felt her presence in the tingle down his spine" (The 1st chakra?). (Parenthetical question mine, *The Shack*, 195)

What do you think? Did Mack, on these two occasions, once in the presence of *Sophia* and again in the presence of *Sarayu*, experience mystical and spontaneous moments of *kundalini*? The indicators suggest he did. I say that if it looks like a duck, walks like a duck, and quacks like a duck . . . it's a duck!

The Immorality of Idolatry

Solomon's introduction of an idolatry that included the feminine-divine changed the human perception of the relationship of the gods with each other, the people with those gods, and the people with people. As the apostle wrote, God "gave them up to uncleanness through the lusts of their own hearts, to dishonour their own bodies between themselves" (Romans 1:24, KJV). With the projection of femaleness into god (*Asherah*, being Baal's consort), in theory it became possible for gods to reproduce gods. So like rats, the gods multiplied themselves (i.e., polytheism).[42] As the gods proliferated and Israel created their likenesses on earth, idols flooded the kingdoms of Israel and Judah. The prophet described the apostasy:

> Therefore thou hast forsaken thy people the house of Jacob, because they be replenished from the east, and *are* soothsayers like the Philistines . . . Their land also is full of idols; they worship the work of their own hands, that which their own fingers have made: And the mean man boweth down, and the great man humbleth himself: therefore forgive them not (Isaiah 2:6, 8-9, KJV; Compare Jeremiah 2:13, 20; 3:1-10, 13.).

For reason of being influenced by the spiritualities of the east—a spiritual adultery which exhibited itself in the people's sacramental liaisons in the high places with male and female prostitutes representing the gods and goddesses—Israel's relationship to her faithful Husband "hit the rocks!"

Relationship on "The Rocks"

Idolism negatively impacted "relationship" among Jehovah's ancient people in two basic ways—first and vertically, their relationship to the Lord was changed, and second and horizontally, their relationships to each other were affected. The people's idolatry impacted both the religious life and social stability of the nation.

For reason of playing the harlot with foreign gods and goddesses (As exhibited in the Ten Commandments, they lived in denial of Yahweh's hierarchical authority over them.), the Lord divorced Himself from the Northern Kingdom of Israel (i.e., the Assyrian invasion and captivity in 722 B.C., Jeremiah 3:6-11). He scattered the nation throughout the ancient world.[43] Like her northern sister, Judah's pursuit of "relationships" with other pagan gods and goddesses also necessitated her eviction from the land. The Babylonians carried her into captivity *circa* 586 B.C. The primal cause for evicting both Israel and Judah from the Promised Land was that both sister-kingdoms played the harlot with foreign gods. Openly and unashamedly, they committed adultery with sacred prostitutes of both sexes before their Husband-Jehovah. They did not understand the hierarchy, the authority, or the fidelity required in their relationship to the Lord (Exodus 20:3). In the Old Testament the Lord showed His people that He was not tolerant of an "open marriage" with them!

But the breakdown of the spiritual relationship between the Lord and His people also impacted the social structure and stability of the ancient Israel. Through Isaiah the prophet, the Lord described the state of affairs: "*As for* my people, children *are* their oppressors, and women rule over them. O my people, they which lead thee cause *thee* to err, and destroy the way of thy paths" (Isaiah 3:12, KJV). Hypothetically, Israel and Judah were two kingdoms *under* Jehovah. But in their idolism, the two sister-nations denied God's authority by creating their own gods and goddesses as they broke God's Law. As a result, the nation's social stability, as Isaiah communicated, lay in shambles.

The Shack's thesis—that the Trinity exists in "a *circle* of relationship," and that "hierarchy . . . is your [humanity's] problem, not ours"—is not only biblically inaccurate (Any concordance check of the word "authority" in the Bible will bear this out.), but also spiritually and socially utopian. Any breach in the concept of God's ultimate authority can lead to spiritual anarchy and moral chaos among God's people. If God, in the governance of family and church, doesn't rule, and consequently and correspondingly neither do the men, then the women and children will. Thus, to the Corinthians Paul wrote, "But I want you to understand that Christ is the head of every man, and the man is the head of a woman, and God is the head of Christ" (1 Corinthians 11:3, NASB). There can be no relationship where there is no responsibility, and there can be no accountability where there is no economy of authority. In fact, one great evidence of the Holy Spirit's filling ministry among believers is *submission* (Ephesians 5:21). Without faithful self-denial, both relationship and fellowship suffer as imperfect people live on this imperfect earth.

Conclusion

Some years ago, a rock singer asked, "What if God was one of us? Just a slob like one of us . . . If God had a face what would it look like?"[44] Thanks to the verbal painting of God in *The Shack*, some may think they have come to see and know the face of God, that he's just a regular sort of guy or girl in whose presence we can even casually cuss if some impulse should lead us to (*The Shack*, 140).

As we pointed out, *The Shack* is big on "relationship(s)." Apparently, to enhance the "relationship" idea for his readers, William Young felt it necessary to inject femininity into the Trinity, a femininity that Scripture neither literally nor metaphorically endorses.[45] But if the femininity of the Trinity becomes ingrained in the collective consciousness of a large number professing Christians, this goddess-ism may lead devout souls into versions and perversions of spirituality utterly opposed by God and His Word. We should remember that verbal paintings can become just as iconic as images carved from wood or smelted from precious metals. As Christians, we should remember that though "we are absent from the Lord . . . we walk by faith, not by sight" (2 Corinthians 5:6b-7).

In our relationship with God, by grace He initiates and by faith we respond. So the question arises, are books like *The Shack* needed to enhance, even initiate, feelings of "relationship" with God? The answer is, not if through faith we have found spiritual completeness in Christ (See Colossians 2:10.). The sovereign God will reveal His presence in us as we walk day-by-day trusting Him, obeying Him, praying to Him, witnessing to the lost, partaking in a the ordinances and fellowship in a local church with other believers.[46] By grace through faith, we receive God's blessings as we become enraptured by His presence in and among us.

We will find spiritual satisfaction through the Savior, the Spirit, and the Scriptures. Through Jesus we experience *contentment* in God. He said, "I am the bread of life; he who comes to Me shall not hunger, and he who believes in Me shall never thirst" (John 6:35, NASB). In the Spirit we experience *companionship* with God.

"The Spirit Himself bears witness with our spirit that we are children of God" (Romans 8:16; Compare 2 Corinthians 13:14.). From the Scriptures we experience *confidence* before God. "These things I have written to you who believe in the name of the Son of God, in order that you may know that you have eternal life. And this is the confidence which we have before Him" (1 John 5:13-14). By resting in Christ, we experience the *comfort* of God. He has promised, "I will never leave thee, nor forsake thee" (Hebrews 13:5, KJV). Such—and much more—is the experiential fruit of being reconciled and related to God, fruit that then becomes the blessing of God through us to those around us.

Sometime during first part of the 1800s, Catesby Paget wrote a hymn, "A Mind at Peace with God." The song contained these words describing the closeness to God that is ours through faith in Jesus Christ:

> Near, so very near to God,
> I could not nearer be;
> For in the Person of God's Son
> I am as near as He.

> Dear, so very dear to God,
> Dearer I could not be;
> The love with which He loves His Son,
> That is His love to me.

Now, that's relationship![47] And it's the relationship of a Bride espoused to Jesus who is "the true God and eternal life" (1 John 5:20). And during this time of our exclusive betrothal to Jesus, our spiritual relationship to Him is closed, not open. There must be no rival suitors.

ENDNOTES

[1] Simon Blackburn, "existentialism, "*Oxford Dictionary of Philosophy* (New York: Oxford University Press, 2005) 125.

[2] Vernard Eller, *The Language of Canaan and the Grammar of Feminism*, (Grand Rapids: William B. Eerdmans Publishing Company, 1982) 37. In analyzing the literary implications of Young's creation of goddess-ism, Eller's "An Excurses on the Unity of God in the Language of Canaan," was most helpful (37-44).

[3] Ibid.

[4] Ibid. 38.

[5] Ibid. 37.

⁶ In the context of God as husband and Israel as wife, we note the phrase "to go a whoring" (Exodus 34:15-16; Deuteronomy 31:16). In acts of spiritual adultery/idolatry, some of which involved physical liaisons with cultic prostitutes, both female and male, God is ever pictured, in spite of Israel's infidelities, as the faithful husband. The phrase "go a whoring" is "almost never used to describe sexual misconduct on the part of the male in the Old Testament." The reason for this emphasis is that the "term is used most frequently to describe 'spiritual prostitution' in which Israel turned from God to strange gods." See Merrill F. Unger and William White, Jr., "TO GO A WHORING, BE A HARLOT," *Nelson's Expository Dictionary of the Old Testament* (Nashville; Thomas Nelson Publishers, 1980) 467-468.

⁷ Illustrating the initiation-response relationship between male and female, and though in our culture this has changed and is changing, in marriage the man usually initiates (i.e., proposes) and the woman responds (i.e., either accepts or rejects the man's proposal). Idolatry represents perversion in that man, not God, initiates it.

⁸ "They attributed their lack of plenty to the discontinuance of honor they paid to the goddess." In other words, the goddess did not respond because they did not initiate. See Vine, W. E., "Queen of Heaven," *Vine's Expository Dictionary of Old and New Testament Words*, (Grand Rapids: Fleming H. Revell) 1981. Online Logos Library System.

⁹ We can only note how in the Word of Faith movement, in the game of name-it-claim-it, God becomes the responder as man becomes the initiator.

¹⁰ In the book's Front Matter, one enthusiast remarks, "Finally! A guy-meets-God novel . . . When I read it, I felt like I was fellowshipping with God." (Mike Morrell, zoecarnate.com) I recognize that Paul Young may sincerely be attempting to promote the relational understanding between God and people. I say "may" because only God knows his intent. However, as evidenced by the connection of the cast of characters to goddess-ism, the author may have additional agendas.

¹¹ Eller, *Language of Canaan*, 40.

¹² Ibid. 40-41.

¹³ Eller, wrongly I think, remarks that, "under the pressures of Canaanite Baalism, Israel failed (or refused) to accept any hint or tinge of such dual-gendered deity." (Ibid. 40). The histories (Kings and Chronicles) and the prophets indicate this was not the case. Both Israel and Judah, as this essay shows, welcomed *Baal-Asherah* with open arms.

¹⁴ I think that the Bible's picturing of God as being masculine better represents His asexuality. After all, by themselves males cannot reproduce. The masculine gender therefore, affirms God's solitariness (i.e., monotheism) and sovereignty (i.e., authority). Infusing femininity

into God deconstructs divine monotheism by imagining a mythological way for gods and goddesses to reproduce (i.e., polytheism), and divine authority by imagining a feminine counterpart equal to Him (i.e., egalitarianism). God's asexuality also possesses Christological implications. It safeguards against the Arian or New Age idea that God's Son was "birthed" in time (See John 1:1.). God's solitary masculinity also voids any thought that a first "Christ" spirit (i.e., Jesus) resulted from the conjugation of primal "father and mother" gods, thereby becoming the first-born of all human spirits. As such, the only distinction between Jesus and us is that the Christ spirit came into being before us. Jesus therefore becomes our elder brother. This primogeniture myth is believed by many New Age spiritualists and cults.

[15] In Canaanite religion, the goddess *Anath* was the female consort of Baal. In addition to being Baal's sister with whom he committed incest, she also served as a prostitute for other gods. As Unger wrote, *Anath* was "given the epithet 'virgin' and 'the Holy One' (*qudshu*) in her invariable role of a sacred prostitute—another illustration of the utter irrationality and moral indiscrimination of Canaanite religion." See Merrill F. Unger, *Archaeology and the Old Testament* (Grand Rapids: Zondervan Publishing House, 1954) 173.

[16] John F. MacArthur, Jr., *The MacArthur Study Bible*, (Dallas: Word Publishing, 1997) 1073.

[17] In a chapter titled "Sex and Possession," Sargant writes: "If man is thought to rise to the level of the divine in mystical experience, it has been believed by millions of people that he can attain the same level in the ecstasy of sex." See William Sargant, *The Mind Possessed, A Physiology of Possession, Mysticism and Faith Healing* (Philadelphia and New York: J.B. Lippincott Company, 1974) 86.

On this point I would note that in the heterosexual-conjugal act, an interpersonal union takes place that is metaphysical, mysterious and mystical. From a pagan point of view, this union could easily be considered as a spiritual linking between humanity and divinity. But Paul warned: "Know ye not that your bodies are the members of Christ? shall I then take the members of Christ, and make *them* the members of an harlot? God forbid. What? know ye not that he which is joined to an harlot is one body? for two, saith he, shall be one flesh" (1 Corinthians 6:15-16, KJV).

[18] "High places housed chambers where male prostitutes and harlots (*qedeshim* and *qedeshot*, Heb.) practiced cult prostitution (cf. 1 Kin. 14:23; 2 Kin. 23:7)." See W.A. Criswell, *Believer's Study Bible* (Nashville: Thomas Nelson, 1997) Online Logos Library System by the Criswell Center for Biblical Studies.

[19] Deena Metzger, "Revamping the World: On the Return of the Sacred Prostitute," *Anima* 12/2 (1986), quoted by Peter Jones, *The God of Sex, How Spirituality Defines Your Sexuality* (Colorado Springs: Cook Communication Ministries, 2006).35.

[20] MacArthur, *Study Bible*, 1059.

[21] Jesus stated that regards marriage, earth and heaven are worlds apart. As a safety net for the woman, the Levirate Law required that a brother care for his deceased brother's wife (Deuteronomy 25:25). Based upon this law, the Sadducees asked Jesus a trick question about a hypothetical situation in which the eldest brother's wife outlived six brothers who had married her to care for her, but predeceased her. In effect, the widow became a hand-me-down sister-in-law as she had been married to six of the seven brothers at one time or another. So the question was asked, whose wife would the woman be in the resurrection—brother one, two, three, four, five, or six? Jesus answered that she would be the wife of none of the brothers, "For in the resurrection they neither marry, nor are given in marriage, but are as the angels of God in heaven" (Matthew 22:30). My point: It's presumptuous to project there's sexuality in heaven because there's sexuality on earth.

For any interested in pursuing this matter further, the Discernment Group invites you read the three-part series posted on *Herescope* titled "Spirituality and Sex," September 19, 23, 25, 2008. See (http:// herescope.blogspot.com/2008/09/spirituality-sex.html).

[22] In John's vision of end-time religion, one can wonder at the system's indebtedness to the divine-feminine as the apostle pictures the goddess holding, "a golden cup in her hand full of abominations and filthiness of her fornication," and having the name, "MYSTERY, BABYLON THE MOTHER OF HARLOTS AND ABOMINATIONS OF THE EARTH" (Revelation 17:4-5). One must also note the violent side of ancient goddess-ism and how this woman is pictured as drunk "with the blood of the saints, and with the blood of the martyrs of Jesus" (Revelation 17:6). Of *Anath*, the incestuous goddess-sister of Baal, Unger notes that she and other ancient goddesses were "patronesses of sex and war—sex mainly in its sensuous aspect as lust, and war in its evil aspect of violence and murder." See Unger, *Archaeology*, 173. My point—ancient goddess-ism possessed a mean streak, and if it did then, it can now, for as the old saying goes, "Hell hath no fury such as that of a woman scorned." In this vein, Scripture portrays the idolatrous queen and false prophet Jezebel as a murderess and seductress (1 Kings 18:4; Revelation 2:20).

[23] Bill Plotkin, *Soulcraft: Crossing into the Mysteries of Nature and Psyche* (Novato, California: New World Library, 2003) 284.

[24] Jones, *The God of Sex*, 47, citing Charles Pickstone, *The Divinity of Sex*.

[25] Rob Bell, *Sex God, Exploring the Endless Connections between Sexuality and Spirituality* (Grand Rapids: Zondervan, 2007) 19.

[26] Ibid. 197.

[27] Neale Donald Walsh, *Tomorrow's God, Our Greatest Spiritual Challenge* (New York: Atria Books, 2004). Supposedly, God tells Walsh: "The words 'Life' and 'God' are interchangeable. When you understand this, you will understand the basis of the New Spirituality . . ." (69) Elsewhere, God told Walsch, "For all of *life* is S.E.X.—Synergistic Energy eXchange." See Neale Donald Walsh, *Conversations with God, an uncommon dialog, book 3* (Charlottesville, Virginia: Hampton Roads Publishing Company, Inc., 1998) 56.

[28] Eckhart Tolle, *The Power of Now* (Novato, California: New World Library, 1999). Tolle wrote, "Adam and Eve saw they were naked, and they became afraid. . . . Shame and taboos appeared around certain parts of the body and bodily functions, especially sexuality. The light of their consciousness was not yet strong enough to make friends with their animal nature, to allow it to be and even enjoy that aspect of themselves—let alone to go deeply into it to find the divine hidden within it . . ." (113-114).

[29] Ryken states: "In the ancient Near Eastern worldview, the sexual activity of human beings, then, is simply an earthly reflection of what takes place in the divine realm." See *Dictionary of Biblical Imagery*, Leland Ryken, James C. Wilhoit, Tremper Longman III, General Editors (Downers Grove: InterVarsity Press, 1998) 776. The dictionary's discussion of "GODS, GODESSES," is also informative (336-340).

[30] Any reader interested in pursuing these matters is invited to read the author's Internet article, "Evangelicals: Emergent *and* Erotic," available at (http:// www. frbaptist.org/bin/view/PastorsPapers/Pastors PapersTopic20090608162318).

[31] Matthew Fox, *The Coming of the Cosmic Christ* (New York: Harper San Francisco, 1988); See also author's *Creation Spirituality* (New York: HarperCollins Publishers, 1991).

[32] Fox, *Cosmic Christ*, 169.

[33] Ibid. 171.

[34] Richard Foster, *Life with God* (New York: Harper Collins, 2008) 113.

[35] "Mark Driscoll and the Sex Driven Church," *Covenant Theology*, April 29, 2009 (http:// covenant-theology.blogspot.com/2009/04/mark-driscoll-and-sex-driven-church.html).

[36] David A. Hubbard, "Ecclesiastes, Song of Solomon," *The Communicator's Commentary*, Lloyd J. Ogilvie, General Editor (Dallas: Word Books. Publisher, 1991) 257-258. Examples of allegory are extant in the New Testament (See Galatians 4:24; 1 Corinthians 5:7; 10:1-11; etc.).

[37] Ibid.

[38] Paul R. House, *Old Testament Theology* (Downers Grove: InterVarsity Press, 1998) 463. Because *Esther* or *Song of Solomon* "do not explicitly quote or mention the name of the Lord at all presents certain challenges to Old Testament theologians," writes House. Such silence also becomes an obstacle for those who try to connect sensuality to God.

[39] Rosemary Ellen Guiley, "Chakra," *Harper's Encyclopedia of Mystical & Paranormal Experience* (San Francisco: Harper Collins Publishers, 1991) 319.

[40] Ibid. 86.

[41] Ibid. 86-87.

[42] It is as if the deities were commanded, "Be fruitful, multiply, and fill the heavens." Hindus believe there are millions of gods.

[43] This scattering has given rise to the myth of "The Ten Lost Tribes of Israel." But the tribes were never totally lost (James 1:1; Luke 22:30). Nevertheless, by playing the harlot, Israel forfeited her relationship with Jehovah, a forfeiture Israel's sister, Judah, did not learn from (Jeremiah 3:10).

[44] Joan Osborne, "What if God was One of Us?" Lyrics at (http://www. lyricsondemand.com/onehitwonders/ifgodwasoneofus lyrics.html).

[45] Obviously, the Father presents a masculine impression to us as does the Son. Over two decades ago, I read an opinion which, supporting feminism, stated theoretically that God's Son could have been born a daughter—this in spite of the prophet's contrary prediction (Isaiah 9:6-7). Jesus also revealed the masculine gender of the Holy Spirit (Greek *pneuma*, neuter). He said, "But when He (*ekeinos*, masculine gender), the Spirit of truth, comes, He will guide you into all the truth . . . He (*ekeinos*, masculine gender) shall glorify Me . . ." (John 16:13-14). *The Shack's* feminization of the Spirit as *Sarayu* contradicts Jesus' masculine gendering of Him. Thus the biblical God cannot be multiplied for reason that He possesses no capacity to propagate Himself. As His creation, we possess His image but not His identity.

[46] I can only imagine how on this point, the super-spiritualists will condescendingly say, "Oh, that's so quaint and out of date. The fashions of spirituality are changing. Poor fellow . . . his brand of spirituality stands out like a polyester leisure suit of the 1960s. Does he really believe such spirituality is all there is? Give us something new to us, something novel . . . something more."

[47] As Paul the Apostle wrote, "But now in Christ Jesus you who once were far off have been brought near by the blood of Christ" (Ephesians 2:13).

CONCLUSION
Breaking Away from Seductive Spirituality

> For I am jealous over you with godly jealousy: for I have espoused you to one husband that I may present *you as* a chaste virgin to Christ. (2 Corinthians 11:2, KJV)

The story possesses the ingredients of a modern day soap opera. She was a well-kept, but neglected and desperate wife of Potiphar, a man who had one of the most demanding jobs in the kingdom—protecting the king's life. Joseph was a handsome, successful, and "unattached" young servant whom Potiphar, head of the secret service, appointed to manage his finances and oversee his household's day-to-day-operation. As Pharaoh trusted Potiphar with his life, so Potiphar trusted Joseph with his wife.

But whiling away the hours of her boring days, Potiphar's wife became restless. She began to feel herself attracted to the handsome and successful household manager. Unable to restrain her sexual "desires," and for reason of her husband's neglect, she came to a breaking point and tried to seduce Joseph. Bluntly, she propositioned him, "Lie with me." But Joseph rebuffed her advances being restrained by the following question: "How then could I do this great evil, and sin against God?" (Genesis 39:7, 9). But when she could no longer contain her desires, and knowing herself to be alone with the young servant, she again forced herself upon Joseph and pleaded, "Lie with me." But breaking from the seductress' grasp, Joseph fled.

This incident from Joseph's life illustrates the challenge faced by godly people through the ages. Appalled at how Israel and Judah had been seduced by Canaanite spirituality, Jeremiah asked:

> Have you seen what faithless Israel did? She went up on every high hill and under every green tree, and she was a harlot there. . . . And I saw that for all the adulteries of faithless Israel, I had sent her away and given her a writ of divorce, yet her treacherous sister Judah did not fear; but she went and was a harlot also. (Jeremiah 3:6, 8, KJV)

And for reason of the world's infiltration into the early church, James protested to the early Christians:

Adulterers and adulteresses! Do you not know that friendship with the world is enmity with God? (James 4:4, NKJV)

So as the Canaanite religion tested Israel's fidelity to Jehovah, the New Spirituality tests the church's commitment to Jesus. Until Christ returns, the seductive spirituality known as, "Mystery Babylon, the Mother of Harlots," will continue her attempts to lure the Bride away from her Groom (See Revelation 17:1-6.).

Thus marriage becomes an appropriate metaphor helping to explain God's relationship to His people, for as Ray Ortlund observes, "God *is* a perfect 'husband' to his people, our sins really are a betrayal of him, and thus a moral category exists for which the image of a harlot is a reasonable fit." He adds that, "when God's love is primarily in view, our 'harlotry' is a meaningful description of our rejection of his love for the love of others."[1]

Peter also warned believers about false teachers who having "eyes full of adultery . . . allure through the lusts of the flesh," and about the devoted masses that "follow their sensuality" (2 Peter 2:14, 18, KJV, and 2 Peter 2:2, NASB). By flirting with seductive spiritualities like those *The Shack* pictures, evangelicals who considered themselves to be "betrothed" to Jesus may abruptly awaken and find themselves to be the "mistresses" of false gods (See 2 Corinthians 6:14-18; please read Proverbs 7:1-27.).

The question arises, why does God tolerate the spiritual adultery of the unfaithful? Perhaps it's because the availability of alternative spiritualities serves to separate true believers from false. As Paul wrote: "For there must be also *heresies* among you that they which are approved may be made manifest among you" (Emphasis mine, 1 Corinthians 11:19; Compare 2 Peter 2:1 which says that, "there will also be false teachers among you, who will secretly introduce destructive *heresies*.").

So the question must be posed: "Are we His bride or a harlot?" It is no wonder that John's last words in his first letter are, **"Little children, keep yourselves from idols. Amen."**

ENDNOTE

[1] Raymond C. Ortlund, Jr., *Whoredom, God's Unfaithful Wife in Biblical Theology* (Grand Rapids: William B. Eerdmans Publishing Company, 1996) 183.